Praise for *The Laws of*

D1169134

"In an age of expensive Sudden Ut... ......
enlightenment, David Spangler is the Prius—a spiritual friend
who will get you there without the high cost and flashy pre-
tentiousness. Decade after decade, David has kept the faith and
resisted selling out to the new cosmetic industry of spiritual
uplift. At once down-to-earth and transcendent, he is someone
you can trust to expand your horizons without sweeping you off
your feet and demanding that you follow him into a cult of the
self-elected avatars of a New Age."

—William Irwin Thompson,
founder of the Lindisfarne Association

"Spangler's *The Laws of Manifestation* is a splendid work of great
spiritual depth. Today shelves are full of books that teach people
how to manifest wealth, health, and love using spiritual laws in
the service of the ego. The gospel of prosperity is all the rage.
Spangler, in contrast, shows that the spiritual laws of manifestation are meant not to serve our voracious consumerism, but to
express our soul's infinite creativity, compassion, and love. When
we act from the level of the soul, we know we lack nothing....
I cannot recommend the book highly enough."

—Jim Marion, author of *Putting on the Mind of Christ*

"David Spangler goes beyond the law of attraction to probe the
deeper principles that connect our personal desires to the unfolding of divine creativity. For those of us who are not obtuse
enough to practice relentlessly positive thinking, he offers an
intelligent alternative—a magic that honors the wisdom in our
worries and doubts, and the transformative power of desire itself.
Both profound and practical, this book is a classic that no aspir-
ing magician should be without. I rejoice that it's back in print."

—Catherine MacCoun, author of
On Becoming an Alchemist

J

The Laws of Manifestation

David Spangler

WEISER BOOKS
San Francisco, CA / Newburyport, MA

This edition published in 2009 by
Red Wheel/Weiser, LLC
San Francisco, CA
With offices at:
665 Third Street, Suite 400
San Francisco, CA 94107
www.redwheelweiser.com

ISBN: 978-1-57863-439-2

Library of Congress Cataloging-in-Publication Data is available upon request.

Cover and interior design by Tracy Sunrize Johnson
Typeset in Bembo

Printed in the United States
MAL
10 9 8 7 6 5

The paper used in this publication meets the minimum requirements of the American
National Standard for Information Sciences-Permanence of Paper for Printed Library
Materials Z39.48-1992 (R1997)

Contents

i

Introduction

Gaian Manifestation:
Beyond Will and Attraction

On my desk is a small figure of Mickey Mouse dressed up in a sorcerer's robe and hat, waving a magical wand, a memento of a long-ago visit to Disneyland. It's Mickey in his Sorcerer's Apprentice role from the movie *Fantasia*. I have it there partly because I love wizards and it's fun to see it, and partly to remind me of what we're moving away from as an objective.

If you remember the movie, the sorcerer's apprentice dreams of himself as a master adept, standing on a mountain top, wielding vast magical powers as all the elements of the world and the cosmos do his bidding. The reality, of course, is that he doesn't know what he's doing and ends up making a disaster with the powers he's invoked.

However, the image of the adept who has inner powers at his or her control with which to shape and move the world is a magnetic one in the imagination of our culture. It's the image of Faust, or even more anciently, that of Prometheus, the bringer of fire—the power of the gods—to humanity. In modern times, this image has metamorphosed into that of the scientist or the engineer, or the corporate CEO, or even the computer geek who has mastered the intricacies of cyberspace and the Internet. It is an image of mastery and power, the ability to translate one's will into tangible effects in the world.

This is a very appealing image to many of us in today's world. The size and scope of modern civilization and the challenges with which it confronts us often make us feel dwarfed and powerless. We talk about "big" business, "big" government, "big" problems, and in the process, we can come to feel very little indeed. The idea of having the power to really shape our world seems out of reach for most of us.

In this context, the idea of manifestation has a definite appeal. It seems to promise a wizard-like power that we may find nowhere else in our lives, the power to shape our destinies, to attract money, real estate, loving relationships, high-paying jobs, diamond necklaces, fabulous health, and whatever else we may want.

The idea of manifestation touches on the most basic of human experiences: desire and the ability to satisfy our desire. Who has not wanted something and not known how to get it? Who has not needed something and despaired of receiving it? What's more, as usually presented, manifestation seems a power that is easy to attain and apply. I don't need a college education, I don't need to work hard, I don't need a special network of high-powered friends or acquaintances, and I don't need a ton of money in the bank. All I need is the ability to imagine and to think positively. Anyone can do that! What could be simpler?

Of course, if that were all there were to it, we would all be living in mansions, money bulging out of bank accounts, driving fancy cars, living lives of sybaritic leisure—or being or doing whatever else pleased us and fulfilled our desires.

The fact that we're not suggests there's more to this picture than meets the eye.

But before looking at the nature and possibilities of manifestation itself, I want to go back to the image of Sorcerer Mickey. Beginning with the Age of Reason in the seventeenth century, on through the Age of Enlightenment a century later and especially with the beginning of the Industrial Era in the nineteenth century, the european image of humanity and its place in the world changed dramatically. It went from a vision of humanity as part of the great chain of being, part of the circle of life, to seeing humans as dominant over creation, bending nature to our will and enterprise. It was during this time that the image of the lone adept wielding vast powers over the world in promethean fashion became such a magnetic one in western culture.

As an image, it fit right into western society's new sense of humanity's role in the world.

But it's a profoundly flawed image of disconnected power, of power wielded without a sense of any larger wholeness or any guiding value other than personal desire and will. The consequences for Mickey are disastrous as he sets forces into motion he neither anticipated nor can control. Likewise, our culture has set into motion forces in the environment that we never anticipated nor can control, with consequences in the form of climate change, rising sea levels, depletion of natural resources, and social upheaval that may be disastrous for us as well.

The image of Mickey the Sorcerer as a symbol of the western image of the adept, whether that adeptship is magical, scientific, financial, or political, is one of mind over matter. It is an image of domination and control. There are situations in which domination and control may be perfectly appropriate and necessary, but generally not with people and not with life or the world itself.

In recent years, a different model has been emerging based on a growing understanding of ecology, systems theory, cognitive biology, and the interconnectedness of life. This model has variously been called "holistic," "integral," or "Gaian" (A tribute to the idea that earth as a whole is a living organism, "Gaia"). Its approach might better be called "mind within matter."

It's the difference between standing outside a system and acting upon it, imposing your will upon it, and standing within a system as part of it and changing it by becoming an active part of its will.

Moving from the first approach to the second is a major shift in thinking and acting occurring in our world today. Increasingly it's apparent that our prosperity and well-being—maybe even our survival—as a species depends on learning how to live holistically in the world. It depends on being a different kind of adept, not one who stands apart but one who stands within in an integrated and coherent way. We need to learn how to "think like a planet." We need to learn how to act as part of Gaia, not as seeking to control and dominate her.

This shift applies to the idea of manifestation as well. The idea of manifestation as simply a way to magically control our world through the power of our intentionality is, if you'll excuse the phrase, strictly "Mickey Mouse" these days. We don't need to be sorcerer's apprentices or all-powerful adepts. We now need to learn what I might call Gaian Manifestation. It is an application of holistic and ecological principles to an ancient art of life-shaping and world-crafting.

This Book

This book is a collection of lectures on manifestation I gave in the Findhorn Foundation Community in northern Scotland over thirty-five years ago in 1971 and 1972. I gave these lectures at a time when the community was growing to ten times the size it had been when I first arrived and there was a real need to understand and practice the principles and processes of manifestation. The survival of the community, particularly as it went from fifteen people to over a hundred and fifty members in a matter of months, depended on being able to manifest, since the community had little money, no economy to speak of (this was before it began operating as a learning and retreat center), and most of the new members were young people in their late teens and early twenties who had no money either.

The three founders of Findhorn, Peter Caddy, Eileen Caddy, and Dorothy Maclean, had learned to manifest as a process of clear imagination and positive thinking. This worked perfectly well when the group was small and everyone could hold the same image of what was needed and could join together in positive thoughts. It became more difficult when the numbers of members grew and grew. Not everyone had either the same training in visualization or the same belief in manifestation as a technique and certainly not everyone could be as unswervingly positive as Peter, Eileen, or Dorothy. Manifestation had served the community well when it had been small, but as the community grew, Peter became concerned that the process would break down.

Because of this, Peter asked me as the one in charge of community education to give a series of talks on the laws of manifestation for the benefit of those who may not have heard of such things and as a reminder to those who had. Peter wanted the community visualizing together and being positive together.

Because of this, this book really is an historic document, chronicling a moment of time in Findhorn's history. The lectures grew out of the need of the community and from questions that Peter or I had been asked. They were designed for a specific group of people at a specific time and place. I didn't think of them at the time as lectures that would one day be published in a book. They were initially collected and published by community members in 1975, two years after I had moved from Findhorn back to the United States. Now, after being out of print for many years, they are seeing the light of day again in this archival edition.

But these lectures are historic in another way. They represent a transition for Findhorn in thinking about manifestation, and for me, they represent my first attempt to articulate what I would now call an incarnational or Gaian approach to manifestation.

In this introduction, I want to give you some of the background that led to these lectures. I also wish to give you my latest thinking about manifestation so that this book has more than just historical interest but offers new insights into what I think of as Gaian Manifestation: the art of co-creative incarnation.

Manifestation at Findhorn

As I have said, Findhorn was founded in 1962 by three people—Peter Caddy, his wife Eileen, and their friend and colleague, Dorothy Maclean. At the time they were unemployed, on welfare, and living in a trailer in a trailer park. To supplement their diet, they decided to grow a vegetable garden on some of the unused land around them. The problem was that this trailer park was built on a beach just off the North Sea. Neither the soil nor the climate were conducive to growing anything more than the scrub grass, gorse, and heather native to that part of Scotland. Nor did they have the money to buy the things they would need. It was a formidable problem. They solved it by using the principles of manifestation.

The miracle of the Findhorn story has been chronicled in many books, so I won't go into detail here. Suffice it to say that over and over again their needs were met by manifestation. Years before as a young man, Peter Caddy had been trained in techniques of positive thinking and visualization, which he called "The Laws of Manifestation." Basically, these principles consisted of holding a clear and precise image in the mind of what one wanted to manifest and then refusing to let any negative thought, worry, or doubt enter one's consciousness. To these two basic techniques, he added steadfastness and clarity of will, a spiritual discipline of attunement, and subsequent obedience to inner promptings, patience, perseverance, persistence, acting in faith, and very importantly, gratitude. Using these principles, the three founders and later the small group who joined them manifested everything they needed, from magnificent gardens to new trailers and a community center.

When I arrived in 1970 as a visitor from the United States, I found to my astonishment that Dorothy, Peter, and Eileen had been expecting me to come. In 1967, wholly unbeknownst to me, they had been sent and had read a small booklet I had published for classes I was teaching in California. After reading it, Eileen had a vision in which she saw me coming to the community and becoming part of its organization. But they had no idea who I was or where I lived. So they waited in faith, and three years later, I showed up. I was, in effect, one of Findhorn's manifestations! The first week I was there, Peter offered me the job of being a co-director with him. I accepted and spent the next three years helping Peter and developing an in-house educational program for the community.

I gave many lectures as part of my work there. Later, after I returned to the United States in 1973 and co-founded the Lorian Association, these talks were collected and published as a series of books. As I said above, this book, *The Laws of Manifestation,* was one of them.

My Personal History of Manifestation

In one form or another, the idea of manifestation has also been part of my life. My parents were friends of the Rev. Norman Vincent Peale and had been married by him. His best-selling book *The Power of Positive Thinking,* published in 1952, had a prominent place in my Dad's library. Faith was an important part of my family background.

When I left home in 1965 at the age of twenty to become a spiritual teacher, I did so as an act of faith. I was following an inner calling that led me to leave college, a degree program in molecular biology, two scholarships, and a laboratory job to become an itinerant lecturer on spirituality. It was a step into the unknown for me, as I had no idea what would befall me or even what it meant to be a spiritual teacher. I called myself a "freelance mystic," and I learned by giving talks and workshops inspired by the spirit within me. It was an exciting time and also a scary time.

As it turned out, for several years, everything and anything I needed to do my work simply appeared in my life as if by magic at precisely the time I needed it, whether it was money, people to help me, or tools to use. For instance, when I felt my work would benefit if I could write and publish booklets for my classes, a gentleman who owned an office supply store contacted me one day and said he felt guided to give me one of the latest models of mimeograph machines plus paper, ink, and other supplies. He would even supply a room that I could use as an office! This offer came totally out of the blue and was an indication to me that I should follow through on my desire to create the booklets. And it was one of these booklets printed on this donated machine that was sent to Findhorn and inspired Eileen's vision which in turn led three years later to my becoming the community's co-director.

On another occasion, I knew I had to stay in Los Angeles and continue with a piece of work even though it wasn't bringing in any income. I had several lecture invitations from other cities, but I couldn't go. My inner direction said I needed to stay and focus on what I was doing.

As the weeks went by, I watched my bank account dwindle. Fortunately, I was given a place to stay rent-free, but I still had to buy food. Finally the job was finished, and I knew I could leave Los Angeles. But by then I had only fifty cents left. That was all the money I had in the world. I had no money to afford to go anyplace else, not to mention no money to buy something to eat!

On the very day my job finished and I discovered I had fifty cents left, I was invited out to dinner by a man whom I had helped. He said, "You've never asked me for money, but you've helped me a great deal. I want you to have this check." It was exactly enough to pay my expenses to drive to Salt Lake City, one of the places that had invited me to come give a series of lectures. I used the money I'd been given to buy gas for my car and headed for Utah. There in Salt Lake, I did earn money lecturing. Most unexpectedly, though, when it was time to leave, a person came forward and said, "I've been inspired by your work and I'd like you to have this check for a thousand dollars." That was more than enough money to get me started again near San Francisco, California, where another group had invited me to visit.

This was an excellent lesson for me in manifestation and trust. I proved to myself that if I did what I needed to do, life would take care of my needs. After all, isn't that what we're taught in various religious teachings? It has certainly worked out in my own life. I know that manifestation works.

However, my approach to manifestation was very different from Peter's. His approach was based on using visualization, will and positive thinking to attract what he needed or wanted. Mine was based simply on manifesting a quality of being and letting life configure itself to me, the way a flowing stream shapes itself around a boulder in the water. It was based on being connected to my own inner inspiration and sense of calling and connected to the world around me. In my terms, manifestation was not about attraction so much as it was about incarnation. There were similar elements in our respective approaches, but there were important differences. I didn't visualize or hold images of what I needed, and for me positive beingness was more important than positive thinking.

Obviously, both our approaches worked. The proof of the pudding, as Peter was fond of saying, was in the eating. Both Findhorn and I were successful at what we were doing. But Peter was interested in how I went about it. As the community grew and it became more difficult to ensure that everyone was visualizing the same way or being equally positive in their thinking, Peter felt that perhaps my approach might complement the way Findhorn had been working and in some ways might even work better. He felt my form of manifestation represented a step beyond what he had been doing. If he was using the "old" laws of manifestation, then, according to him, I was using the "new" laws. He wanted the community to know the difference, and this was another reason behind giving the lectures that are in this book.

I never saw manifestation being divided into "old" and "new" in the way Peter did, although I adopted his terminology for the sake of the lectures. To me, manifestation describes a personal co-creative relationship we each form with life and spirit. It takes a unique form for each of us. In effect, we each need to find what works for us. There is no "new" or "old" about it.

After leaving Findhorn in 1973, I and several other friends whom I had met in the community formed the Lorian Association, a non-profit spiritual educational organization. Through this organizational vehicle, we continued to work together as we had at Findhorn, offering classes and workshops, particularly in the art of creating community.

I continued to think about manifestation on and off, but it wasn't a topic that was at the forefront of my work. I continued to manifest, but it wasn't something that I taught. Several years went by. Then in the late eighties, I was invited by a church in Seattle, Washington, to give a workshop on manifestation.

For the first time since Findhorn, I sat down and began to think about manifestation. What was happening? What were the mechanisms behind the power to manifest? Was it simply a "Law of Attraction," a matter of visualization and positive thinking, or was something else at work? I thought about how I manifested and how Peter did, and the differences between us. I thought about what I had learned through the years about the subtle energy fields that surround us and the process of incarnation.

I put all my reflections and insights together into a program for this church that represented my first articulation of an incarnational approach to manifestation. It proved successful and led to my giving other workshops which in turn led to more thought and reflection and to eventually putting it all down in a book called *Everyday Miracles* which was first published by Bantam Books in 1996, and is now available from Lorian Press.

Years later I refined this technique even more by developing a deck of cards to use in crafting and fine-tuning a manifestation process. I called this the *Manifestation Kit,* and it is currently available from the Lorian Association on our website, *www.lorian.org.*

I continue to explore and develop this topic. For me manifestation is not about a technique. It is about our power as participants in the interactive web of life. It is about who and what we are as generative sources of spiritual and co-creative energy. It is about our capacity to go beyond the imagery of adeptship and power represented by Mickey Mouse as the sorcerer's apprentice to become partners with Gaia, the life of our planet. It's about incarnation and integration, coherency and collaboration. Because of this, there is no end to the learning that is possible about manifestation.

In this introduction, I want to share my latest thoughts on manifestation with you. In this way, this book is more than just a historical document, but an offering of new insights as well, with the hope that they will be helpful and empowering for you.

Beyond Attraction and Positive Thinking

Manifestation is most frequently understood and taught as a power based on a law of attraction and positive thinking. It postulates a relationship between mind and matter that says our thoughts affect the material world outside us in a metaphysical way, attracting to us events, people, and objects that correspond to and mirror our thinking. If this is true, then we want to think positively in order to attract positive outcomes. More specifically, if we have a particular desire in mind, we need to think positively about acquiring or accomplishing it as the power of those positive thoughts is what will bring the manifestation about.

From my perspective and experience, this approach has limitations. For one thing, if I know exactly what I need or want, then visualizing it is a powerful tool. But if I don't know, then visualization may limit my possibilities. There might be many ways a particular need of mine could be met if life has the freedom to present me with different opportunities or possibilities. Peter would say that the good was the enemy of the best and that we should not settle for less than what will do the job perfectly. But sometimes the familiar is the enemy of the possible. We may form images on the basis of what we already know or what we think is possible, neither of which may be the best solution to the need we want to fulfill through manifestation.

Likewise, what is meant by positive thinking? Does a single negative thought of doubt or worry cancel out my manifestation? What about two negative thoughts? Three? Four? How much negativity overcomes the positivity?

An excellent manifestor I once knew was a man who was a perpetual worrywart. He worried about everything. But none of his worries ever came to pass. Though he could be quite negative and pessimistic in his speech and even his thinking, his relationship to people and to life was very open, positive, and loving. And he was usually successful when he set out to manifest something, even though he always claimed that it wouldn't happen for him. He was proof that one thought didn't always attract its corresponding reality. Otherwise his life would have been one disaster after another.

In electromagnetism, likes don't attract at all; they repel. You can see this easily if you try to put the two positive or the two negative sides of a magnet together. In this case, it's difference or unlikeness that attracts. The idea that like attracts like is an observation from human relationships, but even there it doesn't always hold true. Actually, if we think about it, we should be thankful that the so-called "law of attraction" isn't really a law at all, at least not like gravity or the laws of thermodynamics. Imagine if every thought, feeling, or attitude you had actually had the power to attract its corresponding reality in the world. Life would be chaos, or worse. We would certainly learn to discipline our thoughts!

A proponent of the law of attraction could say that not every thought has the power to attract, just as not every magnet is of equal strength, but if the "field strength" is powerful enough, then attraction will take place. I happen to agree with this, but then the question becomes how one determines a thought's power. It's not simply a question of whether a thought is either positive or negative as those who believe in the law of attraction accept that both kinds of thinking attract corresponding consequences. What makes a thought powerful? Is it its clarity? The passion behind it? The conviction of belief?

I'm sure these things all play a part, but we all have examples from our own lives and the lives of others where the most clearly, passionately, enthusiastically held thoughts and images still fail to produce any corresponding result. Yet at the same time, my files are full of stories of amazing manifestations brought about by clear thoughts held with conviction. It happened at Findhorn a lot. Sometimes, it can happen in humorous ways.

A friend of mine was trying to sell her house. She held a clear image of her house being purchased within the time frame when she needed the sale to take place and as part of her positive thinking, she had a prayer-like affirmation that she said several times a day: "Jesus, please sell my house." The problem was that she would get the words mixed up, as we sometimes do, and would say, "Jesus, please buy my house."

She was visiting my wife and me when she got a phone call from her husband saying the house had just been sold. As she got the news, she burst out laughing. I asked her what had happened, and she said, "You know how I kept getting my affirmation mixed up and asking Jesus to buy my house? The buyer is a Mexican-American named Jesus!"

There *is* a phenomenon of attraction that happens in our lives, often manifesting as synchronicities and amazing coincidences, but it just doesn't work all the time or in ways that we always expect. I would hardly call it a "law," but it is something to take into consideration and be aware of. If not a law in itself, it seems to point to some deeper process at work. What might that process be? Like a mystery, we need to delve more fully for clues.

Gaia and Systems Thinking

One clue lies in the nature of the world and in what I call "Gaian" thinking.

I use Gaian as an adjective to refer to an awareness of systems and wholes, just as the planet itself is a whole. The word comes from the name for the Greek goddess of the earth, *Gaia,* and was used by scientist James Lovelock in his book *The Gaia Hypothesis* to refer to the earth as a living organism. To perceive and to think like Gaia is to think in terms of relationships and interconnectedness and what the cyberneticist and anthropologist Gregory Bateson called "the patterns that connect."

A system is a complex whole acting as a single unit but made up of interconnected parts that mutually influence each other in dynamic ways. Our body is a system made up of organs, tissues, cells, and the like. Often, as in our body, the parts that make up a system are themselves systems. Common social systems in everyday life are families, businesses, schools, and governments. The environment is an ecological system.

The key to systems thinking is to realize that a component of a system acts differently when part of the system than when it's separated and observed in isolation.

Taking systems apart to study their parts can give us important knowledge but can never tell us how the system as a whole functions. You can see this in a business. You can interview each employer or manager in the privacy of his or her own home but you still won't have a sense of how the business as a whole operates unless you see them in the context of working together. A person who is a perfect gentleman at home may act as an unthinking tyrant in the workplace, for example.

Systems thinking—what I call "Gaian" thinking— takes into account these complex interactions and dynamics and considers whatever system it's examining as a whole. It is the opposite of reductive or analytical thinking that pulls things apart to consider only the individual components separate from everything else in their environment.

Most goal-oriented thinking tends to be linear, reductive, and analytical in nature, rather than systemic. It focuses upon achieving a particular goal and marshals its forces and logic to do so. In so doing, it may not think broadly enough or systemically enough, and though it reaches the goal, it sets into motion unforeseen consequences in the process. The story of Mickey as the sorcerer's apprentice is a perfect example of this. Further, by trying to fix the problem he created in a similarly linear and reductive way by chopping up the magical broom, he only made the problem much worse as each of the fragments transformed into a new broom that kept obeying the magical impulse to fetch water.

There are many examples in history of this kind of thinking and the problems it creates and especially in our relationship to the environment. Like Mickey, as would-be adepts, we have tried to manage a holistic, systemic, interconnected world in disconnected, linear, and narrowly-directed ways. No wonder we are facing problems of climate change and environmental disorder. What is needed now is to learn to think like a planet, to think in terms of wholes and systems and interconnections: Gaian thinking.

You may wonder just what this has to do with manifestation, but it's very important. All manifestation takes place within interconnected systems. Manifestation is a participation in such systems, but we see it as a linear response of the world to our positive thinking based on an assumed "law" of attraction. The success or failure of our manifestations may have little to do with the clarity of our images or the positivity of our thoughts, and not much to do with attraction either. It may have much more to do with how we connect and interact as part of a complex, dynamic whole system of life.

In the sections that follow, we look at some examples of Gaian thinking with respect to manifestation.

Manifestation as Participation and Co-Creation

Let's assume for a moment that manifestation really does work through a law of attraction. In this view, if you want something, you visualize it, you think positively about getting it, and bingo! Life sends some equivalent of a UPS truck to deliver it to your door. But imagine if you were the only person on earth. How would this happen? Where would my UPS package come from, and who would bring it?

There are things I might manifest that could come to me even if I were the only living thing on the planet. I could manifest joy, for instance. I might have little to feel joyous *about,* but I could still get into a joyous frame of mind, perhaps through a powerful meditation. Mental and emotional states don't really need external conditions to manifest. I can be surrounded with luxury, loving people, beautiful and comfortable surroundings, and I can still feel depressed or lonely. Or I can be roughing it in the woods, with no one around for hundreds of miles, and feel happy and complete and not lonely at all. Everything can be falling down around me, and I can still feel positive and confident; conversely, everything may be going my way, and I can feel pessimistic and afraid. Emotional and mental states *are* influenced by our environment, but they can just as well be at odds with or even divorced from what is happening around us.

Aside from subjective states, everything else we might like to manifest comes to us with the help of others.

Think of something you've received recently either as a gift or a purchase. Think of the chain of people involved in creating this thing and bringing it to you. Would you now possess this thing if these people had not made their contributions to the process?

When we think of manifestation and the law of attraction, we are usually thinking of getting something. After all, it's attraction. But in most cases, for you to attract something, someone else has not only had to participate in making that attraction possible, but they may have had to practice letting go.

Some years ago, I was browsing in my favorite bookstore and came across a book that I had recently purchased. It delighted me to see it on the shelves. It was not one of the big sellers a bookstore would be sure to carry. It was an interesting but not well-known title, and its presence on a shelf in a store was by no means guaranteed. Yet, it was a good book, filled with spiritual wisdom.

As I say, I noted its presence there, then moved on with my browsing. But an impulse brought me back to stand before the volume. It occurred to me that I should buy it. But why? I already owned it, and I'm not in the habit of buying two copies of books (it does happen, but usually not deliberately). I walked away, but again the impulse came, more strongly this time. Eventually I gave in and purchased the book, with no clue whatever as to why I was doing so. It was just something I needed to do.

That evening, I attended a party. There I got into a conversation with a woman who had read some of my books and wanted to talk about them. In the course of this conversation, I mentioned the book I had seen in the store, and she said, "Oh, I've wanted to read that. But I've looked everywhere and haven't been able to find it." Then I knew. I had gotten the book to give to her. I was part of a chain that was enabling her manifestation of this book to occur.

These chains can be tenuous. I could have just said no to buying a second copy of this book, and if I had, I would later have been kicking myself for not following my intuition when I discovered that someone I met was looking for that very same book. It felt very good to be an instrument enabling this woman to manifest something she had been looking for but hadn't known how to find. But for this to happen, I had to let go of my reluctance to buy the same book twice, and then I had to let go of the book itself to give it to her. I had to listen to a vague inner prompting and let go of my disbelief or skepticism of such an intuition. For her to attract, I had to do some letting go.

From this we see that manifestation is a cooperative process. It's generally not something we can do for ourselves without any help, law of attraction or no law of attraction. The involvement of other people is almost always required.

This means that manifestation is a participatory process. We may think of manifestation in terms of what we can get, but we also need to think of it in terms of what we can contribute and how we might make another's manifestation possible. Thinking of manifestation purely in terms of attraction doesn't make us sufficiently aware of this important dimension.

Yet without a spirit of participation, manifestation grinds to a halt or at the very least is obstructed.

Earlier I wrote about a man who was a worrywart and a negative thinker. If the law of attraction was really a law, then he should have been constantly manifesting negative consequences in his life. But he didn't, or at least no more than anyone else does in the course of life's ups and downs. One reason is that he consistently and deliberately made himself available to enabling other people's manifestations. He was a loving, generous, kindhearted person who also happened to be a pessimist. He was always surprised when manifestation worked out for him, as he didn't expect it and was sure that it wouldn't. But it did. He was an excellent manifestor in spite of his negative thinking. The reason is that he was alert to helping others achieve their manifestation goals if he could. He was caring, cooperative and co-creative. He felt that he was part of a larger whole in which the welfare of others was as important to him as his own. This attitude more than made up for his own lack of positive thinking.

Participation and co-creation mean being part of and working within a system, not imposing our will upon a system from the outside. They are examples of "mind within matter," rather than mind over matter. Such cooperation and connection are examples of what I mean by Gaian manifestation.

Manifestation and Patterns

Gaian manifestation has to do with patterns and relationships. As an insight, it can be summed up in this way: we don't manifest anything in isolation. What we manifest are patterns and relationships.

For example, I want to manifest a car. I may not know exactly how a car is going to come into my life but it's something I can clearly visualize and I can certainly think positively about getting a car.

But in fact, I'm not manifesting only a car. I'm also manifesting a relationship to the petroleum industry that supplies the gas I'll use; a relationship to the government that issues licenses and to insurance companies that sell me insurance; a relationship to the infrastructure of transportation, such as roads, and the need for taxes to maintain that infrastructure; a relationship to the service industry that will help me maintain my car, such as mechanics and garages and tire companies. I also need to find a place to park or house my car.

When I manifest a car, I also manifest all these other things. They also now become part of my life. I have manifested a system; by owning a car, I've become part of a transportation system, part of a particular lifestyle.

Or imagine I'm manifesting a spouse. I may in fact attract a wonderful woman or man into my life, but when I do so, she or he brings along relatives, family, past history and connections, friends, a vocation, and so on. I don't just manifest a person, I manifest a whole complex system of relationships that now become part of my life and I a part of it.

Sometimes, this creates problems with our manifestation process. A friend of mine was trying to manifest a car with no success. He came to talk with me about it. I led him in a meditation to attune not only to the image of what he wanted to manifest but to all its potential connections as well. Suddenly he said, "I really don't want a car. I don't support the gasoline industry, I don't like the paving over of the countryside to make roads and parking lots, I don't want to give insurance companies my money. That's why I can't manifest a car. I don't want to manifest everything that comes with it." I then helped him see that what he really wanted to manifest was transportation, which could take different forms. What form might suit him best? "A bicycle," he said. "I really want to manifest a bicycle." The next day he got a phone call from a friend who was leaving town. "I can't take my bike with me," his friend said. "Would you like to have it?" Within twenty-four hours of realizing what he really wanted to manifest, he had the transportation he needed.

Of course, some things we may wish to manifest may not have many connections; they may have a simple pattern. If I want to manifest a toaster, there's not a lot that comes with it. But I do have to have an electrical outlet and I do have to have bread, and a place to put my toaster, so there are some connections there.

But other things are richly connected and part of complex patterns. In such cases, what we are manifesting is not only a "thing" or a "person," but a whole new set of relationships, involvements, and participation in life. We are becoming part of life in a new way, a different way than we may have been before.

Deepening the Image: Beyond Visualization

Thinking of manifestation in such a systemic way affects how we visualize our objective. Most visualization exercises focus on what something looks like. They tell us to "picture in our minds the car that we want" or to "imagine our ideal house" or whatever it is that we're wanting. But if I think in terms of patterns, systems, and interconnections, then everything and anything I manifest is going to be much more than just what it looks like on the surface. It will have its own connections to the world, and it will bring those connections to me in ways which will change me in some way.

For example, a car, as I have suggested, is more than just a car; it's a lifestyle. To manifest a car, we need to understand we're also manifesting the lifestyle and responsibilities that come with a car.

Visualization or holding an image is seen as a key element in traditional forms of manifestation. This is because the thought of a thing is considered to correspond to the thing itself and to attract it. The more clear that thought is, the more precise the correspondence and the more powerful the attraction.

Let's assume as a working hypothesis that this may be true. Then, part of the clarity of the image is not just its form but also what I might call its "systemic identity," the nature of its participation and connections in the larger system of the world. Seeing the object of my manifestation from a Gaian, holistic, systemic perspective will be more accurate than just seeing what it looks like on the surface.

This systemic identity might be very simple or it might be very complex. It may have more connections and potential consequences than we can actually visualize or think of. Visualizing in this systemic way is being aware that what we are manifesting is more complex than just its appearance. I need to have a felt sense, an insight or intuition, on how that complexity enters and integrates into my life.

One way to do this is not simply to ask, "What does the object of my manifestation look like?" We want to ask, "Who do I become if this manifestation succeeds? If I manifest this objective, what do I then look like? What is my new systemic identity?"

When I bring something into my life, I become a new person. I become different. I now become the person with a new spouse or a new car or a new toaster. The change may be very minor or it could be major. Hopefully, entering into a relationship with a life partner is going to have more effect upon me than getting a new toaster!

Seeing in this way brings up a new set of questions which can directly influence the energy and will that I bring to my manifestation. Do I want the changes that this manifestation will bring about? Am I ready and willing to become a different person?

My friend was blocked in his manifestation of a new car until he realized that just visualizing an automobile didn't give him the deeper insights he needed to align his energy behind his objective. The fact was that he didn't like who he would become with a car and wasn't willing to be that person. No matter how clear his image of a car was, his overall image of the actual pattern that he was trying to manifest was fuzzy until he began to "think like Gaia" and look at the level of connections and "systemic identity." Then he could see clearly what he did and didn't want, which liberated the energy of his manifestation, bringing him almost immediately what he really wanted and needed.

I may not know exactly what all the changes may be as a result of my manifestation (who can ever predict that?), but I can have some sense of the possibilities, and I can certainly have a sense of both my willingness and my resistances in the face of those possibilities.

Four Thresholds

For something to manifest, there are at least four elements that need to come together. These are energy, form, environment, and an anchor point. Each of these is a threshold that has to be crossed for something to happen.

ENERGY

Manifestation is affected by the amount of energy we put into it. In physics, energy is a measure of the capacity to do work. *Subtle* energy of the kind that one associates with manifestation, which can be mental, emotional, and spiritual in nature, is more or less the same: it's a measure of the influence or effect a thought, feeling, or spiritual force (or quality) can have in the world. This kind of energy is not the same as what heats our stoves or powers our cars; it's not electromagnetic, chemical, or kinesthetic. But it can still affect or shape the subtle psychological and spiritual environments we all share. For example, subtle energies can affect the mood or atmosphere of a room. A person can be depressed and can fill a room with a feeling of depression without saying a word or showing their emotions in any physical way. Happily, the same is true for joy as well.

FORM

Form gives specification and clarity to the energy of a manifestation. It concentrates that energy in ways that can make it more effective. It provides a connection between our desire and the larger world and creates a channel along which a response can flow.

ENVIRONMENT

Is there an environment that can or will support my manifestation? Am I in touch with that environment? If I'm in a desert and I want to manifest water, it doesn't matter how clearly I specify the form or how much energy I put into my thought and desire, it's not going to happen if there's no water to be had. Something in my environment needs to be willing, able, and present to receive the form and energy of my desire or thought and give it physical manifestation. Otherwise, it won't happen. And I need to be able to communicate my energy and thought to that environment, I need to have some connections in place, or nothing will happen as well. This is an issue of coherency.

ANCHOR POINT

Manifestation is the tangible expression of a connection between myself and the world. Not only do my desires or thoughts need to be clear, but I need to be clear, present, and available in a way to which the world can connect. Think of it like a bridge over a chasm. The chasm is whatever seems to stand in the way of my ability to fulfill my desire or thought. The process of manifestation can bridge that gap, but like any bridge, it must be anchored on both ends. If the world can't "find" me in order to anchor itself in my life, then the gap will not be bridged. Manifestation will not occur.

Let's look at these four elements more deeply.

In manifestation, all forms of energy, physical and subtle, can have an effect. The effect of positive or negative thinking is not so much due to the nature or form of the thought itself but to its energy. A weak, listless, half-hearted thought or feeling is not going to have much effect upon the world around me, even though it may be positive in its nature. An attitude of, "Oh, sure, I can manifest that, ho hum," is not going to get the job done.

But it's not only a matter of the energy we put into a particular thought or feeling, image or desire. Our energy is a whole field. The energy of our thoughts, particularly as sustained over a period of time, comes from the totality of how we embody and hold energy in our lives.

Manifestation is more like a marathon than a one-hundred meter dash. We can have a very strong desire or a powerful intent, and in the moment it's like bursting into a sprint. There's a lot of energy to it, enough to set a manifestation process in motion. But chances are we will not and cannot sustain the energy of that particular thought. Our minds turn to other things; our lives are filled with many more activities, demands, possibilities, opportunities, challenges, encounters and engagements than just this one process of manifestation. But if the desire is integrated into our whole energy field—if it represents and is connected to something deep within us and is not just an impulse in the moment—then the manifestation process that springs from that desire is nurtured by our whole energy field and the entirety of our life.

In the method I teach, particularly as embodied in the cards of the *Manifestation Kit,* I suggest that we think of manifestation as an act of incarnation more than an act of acquisition or attraction. As such, what we are manifesting is really a new version of ourselves: the self we will be if our desire is fulfilled and what we wish to manifest becomes part of our life. I have found this approach helps focus our attention in the manifestation process on our whole life, not just on one particular desire. It's a way of attuning more deeply to the entirety of our energy as a total field within which manifestation takes places.

So while having a positive attitude towards our specific objective is important, we may help our overall manifestation process most by everything we do that keeps our whole energy field—our physical, mental, emotional, and spiritual natures—in good shape. In such a context, a negative thought or worry is much less likely to affect the outcome as long as our energy as a whole remains up and flowing, not just with respect to a particular manifestation but in all the encounters and circumstances in our life.

There's probably not much I need to say about form. Every book or teaching on manifestation I've encountered stresses the need for clear, precise imagery in thinking about what we wish to manifest. Knowing what you want will obviously have more power to it than knowing you want something but you're not sure what. However, there is one point I want to make. If I ask my children what they would like for dinner and they say, "Oh, we don't know, surprise us," that doesn't

give me much to go on. They might not like what I
surprise them with! On the other hand, if they say,
"We'd like filet mignon with braised truffles on the side,
garlic potatoes with Crucolo cheese sauce, vegetables on
rosemary skewers with white bean hummus, and a dark
Swiss chocolate fondue as dessert," this will be beyond
my budget and the resources of my local grocery store.
Either extreme, too little specification of form or too
much specification, can limit or even thwart manifestation. There needs to be some room for life to improvise
if necessary. If my kids say, "Gee, Dad, steak and potatoes sounds great with some chocolate for dessert," that's
something I can do.

This brings us to the issue of the environment.
Manifestation is not magic, creating something out of
nothing. It is the application of natural principles working within a natural world. There is nothing supernatural about it, though it can seem magical at times because
we're generally not aware of the subtle energetic and
spiritual dimensions of the world within which part at
least of the manifestation process operates.

As I said earlier in talking about manifestation as
participation and co-creation, when I manifest some-

thing, it comes from somewhere, usually through the mediation of someone. It doesn't drop into my lap from thin air conjured up by some magical being. If in the environment to which I am connected that which I want doesn't exist or there's no one to act as an intermediary if necessary, then my manifestation becomes much more difficult and much less likely.

By "environment" here, I also mean compatibility and probability. I may live in a neighborhood filled with millionaires, but if I never meet them and am not compatible with the world in which they live and function, then the probability one of them is going to drop by and give me money is very slim. I don't inhabit or connect with their world, so there's no easy avenue of communication, access, or connection. The "compatibility differential" is too high, which drives the probability too low.

Likewise, if I decide I want to manifest a new job as President of the United States, it's theoretically not impossible—any native-born American can hold this position—but if I have no background, no experience in politics, nothing that connects me with the environment of government, executive training, finances, and the like, chances are good this is one manifestation that's not going to happen.

There are different ways to deal with this. One is to make sure I connect to an environment that has a reasonable possibility of holding the answer to my needs. For example, if I want to manifest a relationship, I need to make some connection with an environment in which there are people. This could be engaging with a physical environment, like going out to social events or places where the kind of person I'd like as a friend would be likely to go, or a virtual one, such as meeting people online (though the latter has its own limits). Just sitting at home alone and not venturing forth or making contacts is not going to get the job done.

Another is to explore the linkages—really, the compatibility—between myself, what I want to manifest, and the environments in which I normally live and work. The fewer the linkages or the lower the compatibility, the harder the manifestation becomes.

But environment is not necessarily a deal breaker. One part of the environment is time, and a particular manifestation may simply need time for the environment to change appropriately to make it possible. A friend of mine was trying to buy some special Tibetan bells for her mother but couldn't find them anywhere. No store in town carried them or had even heard of them. So she let it go. But one day a few weeks later she called a friend and a stranger answered the phone. My friend had dialed a wrong number and had inadvertently reached a gift store she had never heard of before. On an impulse, she asked the woman on the other end if she had ever heard of the particular Tibetan bells she was looking for. "Oh yes," the clerk replied. "They're very hard to get in this country but we just got a shipment in this morning!" So my friend got her bells.

The fourth element is an anchor point. In almost all cases this will be us. After all, we're the point around which our manifestation will occur, like the seed crystal around which larger crystals can form as they precipitate out from a supersaturated solution.

The anchor can be our intentionality, our energy, even our participation in life and our sense of abundance and presence. There is a curious passage in the New Testament, Matthew Chapter 25, Verse 29, in which Jesus says (in the New International Version), "For those who have will be given more, and they will have an abundance. As for those who do not have, even what they have will be taken from them." This seems a bit unfair, but it accurately describes a process in which energy generates energy. The more we are part of life and engaged with the world, the more life and the world will engage with us in return.

Manifestation as Incarnation

One way to think of Gaia, the living spirit of the earth, is that it deliberately fosters incarnation. That's what the earth is all about: bringing things to life and enabling them to grow and prosper. A Gaian approach to manifestation, besides being systems oriented and holistic in its perspective, is also incarnational. Its emphasis is on being, connection, and engagement. This is why I feel that approaching manifestation as an act (and an art) of incarnation—of being more fully who we are or who we can be, and of becoming more deeply connected with our world, particularly in loving ways—can only help foster the success of what we're trying to accomplish. It transcends a simple view of manifestation as attraction or as an act of will and gives it a full-bodied flavor, so to speak. It lets us know that we are here to participate in the world and to enhance its well-being, even as we seek to enhance our well-being within it.

Such a Gaian perspective goes beyond Mickey and the sorcerer's apprentice, beyond the old images of adeptship and domination. It allows manifestation more fully to become a spiritual practice, not just a means of acquiring stuff. And it puts us in touch with the deep sources of our power arising from our connections to the world.

I hope you will enjoy the history and ideas represented by the lectures in this book. If you want to explore more deeply my current thoughts and teachings around manifestation, I invite you to visit the Lorian website, *www.lorian.org*. And I wish you well in all your manifestations. May they be the blessing you intend them to be.

David Spangler
JANUARY, 2008

I

Chapter One

What is Manifestation?

Manifestation is not magic. It is a process of working with natural principles and laws in order to translate energy from one level of reality to another. The following are some examples of this process:

An author has an idea. It exists as mental energy. He writes the idea as a play or novel. It now exists in physical form in print.

An inventor has an idea for a new machine. By working with the right materials, he gives that idea physical form.

An artist is inspired by a natural scene: he has a subjective, feeling reaction. This is emotional energy. Through a painting or a craft-work, he gives that idea form on a physical level.

An orator has a concept, which is mental. Through his speech to people, he is able to fire their emotions in response to that concept, say, the concept of free elections. He has translated mental energy into emotional energy.

A piece of coal by itself is cold. Yet, it can burn; it contains the potential of heat. When ignited, that heat is released. Physical energy is translated into radiant heat energy.

These examples tell us certain important things about manifestation. First, manifestation is a change of form or state or condition of being; it is not the creation of something out of nothing. The dictionary defines it as "making clear to sight or mind, making visible." The implication here is that the thing manifested was already there but it was not clear, not visible. It was in a different state of being. For manifestation to work, we are asked to recognize that that which we wish to manifest does already exist, even if it is invisible or separate from our immediate environment. What we seek to do, therefore, is to open a route or start a process through which it can enter our environment and be "clear and visible" to us.

This process may involve faith, which is an abstract and somewhat frightening word to many people, seeming "airy-fairy"; but we need to remember the New Testament definition of faith, given in Hebrews II:I: "Faith is the substance of things hoped for, the evidence of things unseen." The New English Bible phrases it in modern English in a way that directly relates to what we have just said: "Faith gives substance to our hopes and makes us certain of realities we do not see." Thus, the processes of manifestation are rather like ordering something through the post from a catalogue. We do not actually see the thing, but we know it exists and we know the postal laws that will bring it to us.

Being asked to draw to oneself something that exists is quite different from being asked to be a magician and to conjure something up from nothing. It is this confusion of manifestation with something supernatural or magical that blocks many people from using the laws properly. Manifestation is not magic. It is a natural principle or process by means of which something is changed or transferred from one state of being to another.

Second, manifestation deals with a great deal more than just finance, though it is often spoken of within an economic context. The movement of an idea within a person's consciousness from a vague, ambiguous state to one of clarity and understanding is a process of manifestation. One can manifest ideas, states of being, health, as well as tangible objects.

Third, we often think of manifestation as a process of "bringing things down," of giving form and definition to abstract qualities, of making invisible, spiritual things visible and concrete. Yet manifestation can just as easily be a means of elevating and uplifting, of raising the physical into the spiritual. This is often referred to as translation, but it is another form of manifestation. The dictionary definition fails to cover all the aspects of the spiritual definition of this process. Manifestation is the process of translating energy from one level to another, without specifying whether this is "up" or "down" the energy scale. The manifestation of light and heat from coal is an example of translating energy from a lower state to a higher one. The coal becomes invisible, but the heat, which previously was only potential and not experienced, is released and becomes "clear to the mind" or the senses. Likewise, one can translate an emotional or physical experience into wisdom and spiritual insight, which is transferring energy from a lower to a higher level of awareness and appreciation.

This illustrates a fourth point, that manifestation is a process of releasing a potential. This is another way of saying that we are manifesting what already exists. The heat was potential within the coal. The answer is potential within the problem. Health is potential within illness. Abundance is potential within poverty. Divinity is potential within humanity. Manifestation is a means of bringing the reality of potential into the reality of actuality, availability, and activity.

The fifth point, which our examples show, is that manifestation is not something that is highly esoteric or spiritual, a complex process that can be worked by only a few special people. It is something we all do all the time through our thinking, our feeling, our actions, our very living. One important way in which we do this is through our speech. Language is a tool and example of manifestation. It is the giving of form through sounds and letter shapes on paper to energies of mind and feeling, and of the spirit as well. Speech is a primary creative tool, an energy of manifestation itself, which is why spiritual teachers have always bade us to be aware of our language, of what we say and how. We are always manifesting when we talk, and the forms we make visible to others through our speech can reveal much about our own inner states; they can also determine the nature of the world that we experience and what we attract to ourselves. This is the reason for the oft-repeated suggestion to keep our speech pure, clear, and positive, as well as sacred, using the power of language economically so as to conserve and magnify its power. How often we hear it said of a person that he does not say much, but when he does everyone listens. We also hear the opposite of some others that their superfluity of speech cheapens and dilutes the strength of what they say and makes them simply boring, dissipators of energy. This is also the reason to avoid purposeless, negative talking. If we dissipate our powers of manifestation on one level, or turn them to negativity, then we dissipate or negate them on many levels; an abundance of speech may lead to a poverty of manifestation.

This importance of language to the understanding of the processes of divinity and manifestation is underscored by spiritual teaching. At the beginning of the Gospel of John, we read: "In the beginning was the Word, and the Word was with God and the Word was God." Likewise, in the passage on faith in Hebrews, II:3, we read: "By faith we perceive that the universe was fashioned by the word of God, so that the visible came forth from the invisible." God manifested through the power of His language, the speech of divinity. We also manifest through our language, the language of speech, of thought, of feeling, of expression, of action, of being.

We are always manifestors. Understanding this can help us to be manifestors of that which we really want within our lives and the life of our world.

In essence, the clue to manifestation lies in the recognition that God in His wholeness is the only reality. Everything in the universe is directly or indirectly related to everything else through this wholeness and there is no barrier or impediment of time, space, or circumstance that can obstruct the right flow of energy between affinities within the whole. As I think in my heart, so I am; as I am, so I create my world, attract my environment, manifest my being in relationship to the whole. God is all there is. In Him there is no lack. He is reality. The more a consciousness can perceive and understand this and live within this reality, the more he can work the laws of manifestation successfully on every level and in every circumstance of his life. Through oneness with God, I am one with all things, and through this oneness I can be the Supreme Manifestor.

This is what manifestation is: the working of natural laws of energy exchange and transference within a consciousness of the whole and through an attunement to the presence of the wholeness, God. It is not a passive state, an attitude of complacent waiting, assuming that life will attend to all one's needs. It is not a magical operation. It is a dynamic state of consciousness. On human levels, manifestation does not replace working for a living; it is simply a different way of expressing the livingness of the work and the work of living, where work is truly seen as "love in action."

2

Chapter Two
The Levels of Manifestation

Man's consciousness functions on different levels, and the way in which an individual perceives and interprets life and the universe depends on which of these levels or combination of levels predominates in forming basic attitudes and ideas. Where the consciousness is orientated will determine how the individual will understand and work with natural law. Although the essence of manifestation is basic to all levels of life, how the processes of manifestation are approached and utilized, the mechanics of manifestation, depends on a person's level of consciousness. An understanding of this throws light on what is meant by "old" and "new" laws of manifestation.

There are four levels of manifestation and of the consciousness to work its laws:

The **physical level** is experienced by everyone and it represents our most obvious level of manifestation. On this level, physical energy expended through some form of labor is the means used to bring manifestation about. We call this working for a living. For example, to manifest bread we plant wheat seeds, grow the wheat, harvest it, process it into flour, make the bread dough, bake it, and so forth. We now use machines to expedite many of these stages, but machines also are a form of physical energy. Money is a symbol for physical energy that also expedites the manifestation process by simplifying or eliminating the system of direct bartering of concrete goods.

On the physical level we work very obviously with laws in order to accomplish manifestation. These are natural, economic, religious, and social laws. We do not consider them to be supernatural. Natural law dictates that wheat, not corn, will come from wheat seeds. Economic and social laws describe the flow and manifestation of money, prestige, and culture. Religious laws tell us how we must behave in order to manifest the "good and righteous life." The source from which manifestation comes is also seen in terms of these laws: we acquire what we want from nature, from the economy or society, or from God through these laws and because of them. These laws represent the "middle man" between ourselves and the Source, the means by which we can relate to and receive from the Source, after having expended the appropriate physical energy.

On the religious side, an example of this is seen in the doing of good deeds or good works in accordance with the precepts and laws of a particular religion in order to receive blessings from Deity. God is seen and understood through His laws, and our relationship to Him is one of obedience to His laws within our physical life. Thus, we may be enjoined to eat certain things but not others, to wear certain kinds of clothing, to do certain things on certain days or at certain times of the day. Faithful observance of these physical rituals will result in a manifestation of divine favor.

In any area, these laws are concrete, dealing with tangible, demonstrable, observable realities and processes and can be understood and related to by consciousnesses conditioned by the concrete, form nature of physical life. Manifestation by means of these laws does not require an abstract or speculative awareness; only a willingness to expend physical energy through the appropriate form of work and labor.

The process of manifestation is given a new dimension when the energies of the emotional realms are added. Naturally, thought and feeling are involved in most kinds of physical action and work, generating the incentive, the desire, the direction that can stimulate and channel physical labor. As we are using it here, however, the **emotional level** of manifestation refers to the use of feeling energies directly and physical energies indirectly in order to bring about a desired condition within one's environment. This often involves the manifestation of things which seem beyond the scope of our physical endeavours. This might be the manifesting of health when physical medical attention is not available or is ineffective; this is "faith healing." It might also be the manifestation of needed supplies when the apparent resources available to be tapped through physical work are not sufficient. An example of this would be a case where an individual needs a sum of money more quickly than he can raise through earning it, or perhaps beyond the reach of his salary. Following the injunction in the New Testament to "ask, and it shall be given unto you," and with an attitude of faith in God's abundance, the person places his need into prayer, then releases it. Subsequently he may receive a check from a relative or friend, an unexpected gift that meets his need. Or he may be prompted to read something or go somewhere or meet someone, and through this is put in contact with an opportunity to earn the money.

The operative factor in this kind of manifestation is faith and the energy of devotion. God is seen as a loving parent, a father (or mother), who knows the needs of

His (or Her) children and can supply those needs. Prayer or affirmation, faith in God, and an openness to God constitute the "working" of the laws of manifestation on this level. This does not replace the physical level; faith is not a substitute for work within the concrete world. Instead, it enhances labor and expands its effectiveness. Where there is faith, there is trust, security, and a lack of tension or worry; work becomes a joy, and one is more open to being guided into the kind of labor that is truly fulfilling.

Keynotes to this level of manifestation and the consciousness required to work its laws may be found in the Sermon on the Mount, Matthew 6:28-30; 7:9-11.

> Consider the lilies of the field, how they grow; they toil not, neither do they spin and yet I say unto you, that even Solomon in all his glory was not arrayed like one of these. Wherefore, if God so clothe the grass of the field, which grows today and tomorrow is cast into the oven, shall he not much more clothe you?"

> What man is there of you, who if his son asks for bread, will give him a stone or if he asks for a fish, will give him a serpent? If ye then, being of human limitation,

know how to give good gifts unto your children, how much more shall your Father which is in heaven give good things to them that ask Him?

Faith in God, our Father, and placing our requests in prayer to Him, knowing through faith that He will meet our needs, thus releasing the problem to Him: this is the essence of manifestation through devotion and the energies of the emotional level.

One other point should be mentioned here. The energy of emotion is the fuel for this level of manifestation; this energy can as easily be expressed as desire and fear as it can be expressed as faith. Thus it may be used for negative results. Worry can be as potent a form of faith as prayer and can trigger the laws of manifestation with consequent effects of an undesirable nature. The laws of manifestation on this level are neutral and will draw to us according to the seeds of desire, belief, and attraction that we plant.

Faith is quite different from hope. The former partakes of knowing and is consequently powerful, able adequately to release the energies required for manifestation to take place. The latter partakes of not-knowing. It is not a single-pointed expression of consciousness, for it admits of fear and an acceptance that perhaps manifestation will not take place. This lack of unity dissipates energy, providing no fuel for the engines of manifestation. Faith, by contrast, is one-pointed knowing.

This one-pointedness, or concentration, is a key to manifestation, as indeed it is to all forms of creativity. Compare the difference in force between a spray of water covering a wide area and a stream of water concentrated through a hose in one direction. The ability to give definition and form to energy is essential to manifestation on the planes of form (body, emotions and mind). It is, in fact, essential on all levels but particularly where concrete manifestation is required, for obvious reasons. Concentration and direction greatly magnify the power of subtle energies to effect changes on physical levels. True faith is such a concentrator of emotional energy, raising it to a high level of affirmation and potential activity and influence.

When to faith one adds knowledge, then the power of concentration is enhanced manyfold. The mind is the instrument of concentration, definition and form-building in the subtle realms, particularly through the power of the imagination. When this instrument is plugged into the powerhouse of emotional energy and faith energy, then the powers of manifestation are greatly increased. The ability of using the mind to create the channels of positive thought and directive imagery through which the subtle energies can flow with magnified power for being thus concentrated is the essence of **mental level** manifestation.

A child, in order to be fed, clothed, housed, and cared for, need not know what kind of job his parents have, nor the details of their work. It is sufficient that he knows their love for him and is secure in knowing that through that love his needs are met. As he grows older, though, a greater knowledge of the working of the family and of society, of the laws by means of which the family itself manifests its needs (and from which manifestation his needs are met), is necessary to prepare him to take his responsible, adult place in the world and to build a family of his own. It becomes no longer sufficient that he simply acknowledges his parents with respect and love, and trusts in their care; he must learn the principles of life under which they work and apply them himself. His attention is shifted from seeing his parents as source to seeing the workings of the laws by means of which his parents accomplish their manifestations, that through understanding and participation he might realize within himself the qualities of the Source.

This step in the life of a child is equivalent to the step a soul takes when it begins to learn the laws of mind and to apply them so as to enhance the working of manifestation. On this level, the image of God, the Source, is less that of being a parent and more that of being Universal Mind. Further, man sees himself less as a child and more as an emanation of Divine Mind. Blind faith, though powerful and effective in its way, still often sees God and man as separate beings, with the latter dependent on the former. In this, faith has an inherent limitation. In learning the proper use of the mind, however, man becomes increasingly aware of his own divine powers and of his essential kinship with God. The unity and oneness of the universe becomes more real. The Hermetic axiom, "As above, so below" becomes a key to knowledge, enabling man to find correspondences between the laws of the universe and the laws of his own being, enhancing his understanding and utilization of both.

With this awareness of inner divinity and of working in harmony through one's own mind with the laws of divine, universal mind, the techniques of manifestation on this level revolve around the right use of thought. Thought is the process of creating images and forms on the mental plane; these forms (which may be concepts, pictures, or words) can then be used to concentrate and direct energy and to liberate the power of will. On the level of the personality, will is the result of an energy flow concentrated in a one-pointed fashion. Will need not be generated through tension; in fact, straining will dissipate energy. Will is generated through the relaxed yet single-pointed use of the imagination to form an image and to summon all the forces of consciousness to flow into and through that image for a certain period of time. Will is a force but it is a force created through concentration, not through pressure or strain.

This is very important to understand, for willpower is regarded as a key element in the processes of manifestation as directed from levels of the mind. True will is not force or pressure in its nature, though it may be forceful in its impact. Where pressure exists as a source of will, one can also usually find a sense of fear, insecurity, or doubt that a certain manifestation will take place. This makes the individual "turn on his will" in order to try to force events; then will is used as an energy of domination, of trying to bend events, people, or circumstances to one's will, even when that will may he used in service to God.

The true willpower that lies behind effective manifestation is based on knowing absolutely that a certain manifestation will take place. In this, it is like true faith. This gives a sense of serenity and peace, of non-reactive inner stillness which can therefore be a source of great power, for no dissipation is taking place. This flow of power can then be concentrated through the vehicles of mind, emotion, and body. It is this concentration that reveals the will, giving it its often irresistible qualities and its appearance of great force. The essential nature of this kind of willpower is that it does not dominate or manipulate: it clarifies and vibrates through a situation, making possible the revelation and unfoldment of the perfect divine pattern inherent in that moment. It strikes a note to which lesser sounds can align themselves to form the chord of manifestation. It is like a magnetic field around which iron filings can arrange themselves. It is like a sound wave that causes sand particles to form geometric patterns corresponding to the crystalline properties' potential within them. This concept of the unfolding and revealing quality of will may be compared for deeper understanding with what was said earlier about manifestation itself: it is a means of turning potentiality into actuality by drawing out of a situation or person a deeper or higher aspect that was inherently there all the time but obscured by the outer appearances.

Another useful seed-thought for further meditation is the esoteric association of the energy of divine will with the creative spirit and essence of beingness itself. That quality which, in one of its aspects, we call "will" is at the core of existence itself, lying at the heart of the mystery of divinity and of the primal manifestation of creation.

The energy of will, brought into play through right concentration, is at the center of all manifestation on every level. It is the seed of being around which all else can coalesce and take form. On the mental level, this energy is brought into play through right thinking, through positive thought, the use of the imagination to form clear, precise images, through one-pointedness (which, in group work, means unity of the group mind and imagination) and affirmation. Manifestation is effected through the mind of man working in harmony with these laws of universal mind.

The next level of manifestation is the **soul level.** This is the dimension of the New Age consciousness. Before discussing it, however, there are still certain points to clarify concerning the dimensions of mind, emotion, and body. Together, these make up the personality level. In esoteric concepts, the personality is not the identity nor the individuality, though it thinks it is; it is actually a complex of energy which provides a certain kind of learning and growing environment (in some ways like a greenhouse) within which the true individuality may unfold. A characteristic of this environment is that it divides the universe and beingness into an inner and an outer reality, a subjective and an objective state. In other words, the veil of the personality separates creation into "Me: What I Am" and "It: Everything Else." This sense of personal reference causes the soul to experience creation and life with greater intensity leading to greater self-realization.

Thus, from the level of the personality, we experience our world through a subject to object relationship. We do not so much come into oneness with other elements in our world as that we form combinations of relationships with them, creating complex forms. We own things, are near to things, are distant from things, work with things, but always our experiences are colored by our basic sense of separation through our personality from everything else.

Even so-called "personality affinities," if expressed only on personality levels, do not represent a true oneness, only an intimate combination.

Manifestation as expressed by the personal becomes an exercise in the invocation of things (including people) which are understood as being external to the individual. This means that a sense of separation, even of lack, underlies all forms of manifestation operated by a personality-orientated consciousness. We are manifesting things which are separate from ourselves and which we do not have at the moment—otherwise, why would we be manifesting them? This may not be a despairing sense of lack; we may know how to get something. Nevertheless, we begin with a basic idea that we are separate from the thing or person we want. This is true even when we are manifesting subjective states of consciousness. When we begin the process of manifestation, we feel a lack of the consciousness we are seeking. It is only later, as we begin to experience and grow into the newer state, that we realize that lack was only an illusion, that the consciousness we sought was within us and part of us all the time, only obscured by personality factors. In this sense, we might say that many forms of manifestation (if not all) consist really of a process of stripping away that which prohibits or clouds realization of what is there, rather than in drawing something to us. The core of "working the laws" is basically an overcoming of the illusion of separation, an overcoming of the limitations of the personality consciousness.

Before the individual can understand the deeper processes of manifestation (which relate to the very nature of his beingness and divinity as well), much less use those processes to the fullest extent that is possible, he must transcend the limitations of the personality self. Manifestation is essentially a means by which God expresses Himself. It is revelation in action, rather than a means through which one can acquire things, which is how the personality consciousness (even with the highest of motives) tends to interpret it. To "work the laws" of manifestation is to participate in divinity and should be an experience of deepening soul contact and understanding, not only a method on outer levels causing the attraction and precipitation of desired items, but more importantly, revealing more to the individual about his basic divine nature, his oneness with the whole. Seeing manifestation as simply a means of "getting things" is to rob the process of its vital meaning and educative power to transform consciousness and to make it only a shallow process of power manipulation of events and things.

To open up the greater potentials of both the divine consciousness of the individual and the laws of manifestation as they emanate from and express the beingness of that divinity within the soul requires transcending the separated personality self and moving into the consciousness of the whole. Thus, to move from the level of personality manifestation, using the laws and energies of the physical, emotional, and mental realms, an individual must understand and apply certain bridging principles which will lift him to the level of the soul.

These principles are basically those which deal with the giving up of the energies of self-will, of loosing the bonds of the personality complex which are formed through desire, and of learning to merge oneself into the consciousness and rhythm of the whole of creation. This corresponds to the process of the fourth initiation, the death of the personality, and the rebirth of individuality into the greater body and life of the soul. It is also symbolized in Jesus's life as the Gethsemane experience, expressed in the words, "Not my will, Father, but Thine be done." Thus, these bridging principles involve the giving up of the personality self, the transmuting of self-will and desire into the vision, motivation and will of our soul's divinity. It is learning to put God and the whole first, and through this, coming to learn of one's inseparable identity and oneness with the whole. It is learning to love as the whole loves its parts, not as separate elements but as unique elements within a single unity.

As these principles come to live more and more within a person's consciousness, he begins to participate increasingly in the viewpoint and attitude of the soul. The soul is group conscious. Though aware of its unique individuality as a center of divinity, the soul is also aware of the essential energies of unity that sweep through creation. It perceives distinction and difference, not division and separation. Further, just as a basic need of the personality is to attract and to acquire, the basic need of the soul is to serve. The personality is the instrument through which the individuality draws nourishing experience to itself; it is an agent of inbreath, speaking generally. The soul is the instrument through which the individuality externalizes and reveals its divine nature into the realms of form; it is a vehicle of outbreath, of causation. Thus the soul is also called the **causal body,** with intuition being its basic mode of perception.

These differences between the personality and the soul profoundly affect the attitude toward and the utilization of the processes of manifestation. A certain intuitive insight—a reading between the lines—is necessary to understand **causal** or **intuitive** manifestation, for language does not contain concepts to describe this level accurately. Certain key words or phrases can be used as seed-points for further meditation, but some form of illumined thinking, "tuning in," or meditation is required, for the intellect alone cannot fully grasp the working of dimensions which are "above" it.

There are certain things that can be said which will suggest what intuitive or soul manifestation consists of. In the first instance, the consciousness that is conducting manifestation from this level is at least tuned into the perception and viewpoint of the soul. The soul perceives oneness. It sees others not as separate entities but as its self manifesting in a different form. Thus, the soul forms what we could call subject to subject relationships. In relating with the universe, it is relating with itself, and it knows it.

This leads naturally to the realization that the soul does not experience lack in the way that the personality does, as a sense of separation from a desired object external to itself. Consequently, manifestation to the soul is not a means of attracting that object. What the soul does experience is potentiality and actuality, and the work of its consciousness is to transform the former into the latter, to externalize from its divine center the qualities of that divinity and to express them through form. The need and interest of the soul consciousness is not how to draw things to itself from the environment but how to draw out from itself the qualities and energies from which a greater environment can emerge. The process of manifestation becomes one of externalization and realization; it is one of giving, not of receiving or taking; of revealing and releasing, not of attracting. The soul is not a center of invocation but of evocation; it is like a portal through which the Divine can emerge, can move from one level of reality to another. As long as the soul is radiating its energy of being in this fashion, giving out in manifestation of what it is in actuality and potentiality, then it is being true to its creative nature. Energy is released which will automatically build up about the individual complementary and supportive patterns which meet the needs of unfoldment for that soul. This is the energy of will.

We have already discussed that will-energy lies at the core of creation and manifestation. It is the emanation from being itself. Its nature can be suggested in the statement, "as a man is, so does he create his world." Whatever we do on any level must reflect in some manner our nature upon that level. For example, we can often judge what a person is like by the environment in which he lives, the way he decorates his home, the clothes he chooses, and so forth. Will is the energy that motivates creation and naturally what we create is always a reflection in some fashion of what we are or think ourselves as being or, for that matter, are trying to make ourselves become.

The source consciousness of will energy is the consciousness that knows "I AM THAT I AM!" It is born from the divine center of wholeness; thus, will is never separative in its essence, though it may be destructive in its impact upon form, destroying that the life within may be released to grow. Will does not act from a center of energy upon external things; will does not manipulate within a subject-object context through force or domination. The true energy of will manifests the power and rhythm of beingness, and everything that is attuned to that quality or characteristic of rhythm will be attracted and will align itself accordingly. Will creates through revealing the nature of the Source and the Center, the ultimate authority. Rather than acting as a pressure upon the surface of things, it acts as a magnet drawing the comparable divine nature from out of the heart of things.

Will is a causal energy, not a reflected one. By this is meant that the energy of will proceeds from itself, from the essential character of the being that is its source; it does not proceed from reaction to external experiences coming to that being. For example, if I know I cannot eat a certain kind of food which I like and it is served to me, I say that I have to use willpower to refuse to eat it. What I am really doing is to use a force to separate myself from something that I am identifying with through desire. This is not true willpower. True will is born from right identification. If I do not identify with the food in question, if I stop desiring it and seeing it as a part of me, then I automatically can pass it by. This involves no strain, no tension of refusal and frustrated desire. It is an affirmation of being. Another example would be when a person reacts to obstacles that prevent him from reaching his goal and uses his will to push through them, feeling the tension of the overcoming. There is no tension involved in the use of true will, for there is no tension involved in being oneself.

The reason that most people do not have access to the true energy of will to use in enhancing manifestation on all levels is that they do not know who they are. Will, we said earlier, proceeds from concentration. To the soul level, energies are concentrated through identification, the knowledge of "Who I AM." When consciousness is confined to mental, emotional, and physical levels, it is surrounded by many forms of energy and life, about itself and within itself. The problem of identity is acute. Men use willpower as a means of trying to discover and affirm identity, for it has been long recognized that a man who knows who he is has a self-assurance and a power that others do not. The reason is simple: his energies are concentrated around that sense of identity and its expression and are not dissipated through conflicting self-images. If creative power can be liberated by a strong sense of personality identification, imagine the power released to the person who knows his soul self, his divinity, his changeless I AM. When people are faced with temptation and must use will to overcome it, in reality they are still attempting to decide who they are—what is part of their being and what is not. When a person knows himself and knows the energies that are attuned to him within creation, then he is not tempted. He draws or manifests to himself only that which is in reality an extension of him.

It has been said that the secret behind intuitive manifestation is simply TO BE. This is true, but this must be understood as referring to "SOUL BEING," the state of consciousness that is one with the whole, one with God, one with its greater self. The personality is a collection of ever-changing states of being, reflecting the energies of the environment as the individual re-acts to the world about him. One must use the fire of discriminatory light and will and intelligent wisdom to determine the nature of one's real beingness and to affirm it, through discipline casting all else aside. This is not creating separation, for discrimination leads one to the heart of essential beingness, where the individual is at one with all things. The person who accepts everything as being right and admits any experience into his life is a tool for he is confusing acceptance of all things with being the oneness at the heart of all things. Failing to discriminate on the level of form, he may lose attunement to the level of true substance and essential reality. In so doing, he cuts himself off from himself and from the source of his greater manifestations.

To sum up this discussion on soul level manifestation, it should be realized that we are dealing with a level that is abstract and beyond static forms, a level where the consciousness and the energies it expresses are more attuned to pure being and identity and are relatively free-flowing. Yet to tap soul levels, one must have a soul-attuned consciousness.

One cannot reason or think one's way to such attunement. Logical analysis and mental processes can only take one so far; then one must launch, through meditation, into formlessness. One must allow one's soul, the presence of the god within, to speak to one, not the other way around. The energies of the soul are not there at the disposal of the personality; indeed, they only become fully available when the personality is attuned to soul consciousness. The key to these levels lies in "seeking first the kingdom of heaven," of putting God first, of seeking to attune to His will, which is, of course, the same will and spirit of being that is each person's own true identity, the I AM THAT I AM.

The personality attracts things to itself through manifestation; the soul unfolds the divine presence, using manifestation to create forms that give God birth. The personality attunes to the surface and shapes and forms of things; the soul attunes to their essence, with which it is at one, and manifests that essence through identification and attunement. This essence then creates its own form upon mental, emotional, and physical levels. Thus, the individual becomes not a center of attraction but a portal, a center of evocation, of revelation of being, through which the presence of the whole, God, can manifest Himself.

In this way, the source of manifestation is seen as the oneness, the state of identification between the soul and God. This is cooperative creativity. It is "synergetic divinity" through which the unity of individual soul plus the whole creates a revelation of divinity which neither could accomplish separately.

3

Chapter Three

The Old versus The New
Laws of Manifestation

The growth of Findhorn has largely been based on the application of the laws of manifestation. For many years these laws were expressed as follows: Give up all of the little self so that one can have a clear vision of the will of God and of what constitutes a true need and not simply a personality desire. Look to God and God alone to meet that need. Have a precise vision or idea of what is to be manifested, if necessary sharing that vision so that all involved in the process have the same idea and are united in their thought and imagination. Ask once, knowing in faith that the need is being perfectly met. Give thanks that this is so and release it. If action is required, go ahead in faith, keeping in mind the positive thought and image of the need being met. When the manifestation occurs, give thanks again. Realize that what you have manifested is not your possession but is part of God placed under your care and trust. Treat all you have as if you were their custodian, willing to release them when their work is done. Care for all you have with love and skill, recognizing them as gifts from God.

There is no question that the laws of manifestation, expressed in this fashion, work. The mode of operation used and the principles and energies involved are largely a combination of emotional and mental levels, with physical action as required. There is positive thought, precise formation of mental images with the consequent concentration of energy, faith and the bridging principle of putting God's will first. At the same time, the individual remains within a subject-object relationship with his world. He is consequently invoking things external to himself, the presence of which he does not recognize within his being or environment and which therefore constitute a lack and need. He is working with God as principle, law, father, yet still in some way as a source external to himself; and he is asking for things, acting as a center to which things can be attracted, rather than being the essence of all things and acting as a center of evocation through which the wholeness (that essence) can externalize itself into the appropriate forms. He is trying to draw something from God, rather than working with God to give something new form and expression. This kind of consciousness thus tends to see manifestation as attraction, abundance, and need in terms of multiplicity and form, itself as a receiver instead of as a creator, and in general is maintaining a personality rather than a soul awareness. Expressing a personality orientation, no matter how noble or refined, there is always a chance that a feeling of lack, of anxiety, or of pressure can creep into the processes of manifestation and consciousness, creating obvious or subtle states of tension within the individual, filling the experience with consequent and unwanted strain and stress.

The "New Laws of Manifestation" represent the processes of manifestation conducted from soul levels and are intended to encourage individuals to raise their consciousness to that level and to overcome the limitations mentioned above. Inherent in an understanding of these new laws is a redefinition of the terms, "abundance," "need," and "manifestation."

Abundance

Viewed by the personality, abundance is a measure of quantity. It means plenty, a multiplicity of things and forms. To the soul, however, abundance is a quality. It means the One Essence within all things, from which all things spring. To have a consciousness of abundance, on a soul level, does not mean having a sense of access to many things, seemingly stored in some treasurehouse, but rather being at one with the essence behind and within all things. True abundance is a consciousness of wholeness, oneness, and quality, not of separateness, multiplicity, and quantity.

Need

Too often we think of needs in physical terms as things or as people. While in practical fact this may be valid, it is still a limitation that can have effects on our state of consciousness and our understanding of manifestation. First, by seeing needs as forms which we must manifest, we equally see them as forms which we do not have. This encourages a sense of lack, an acceptance of "not-having" that prevents our attunenment to a consciousness of abundance. Second, by defining manifestation, as many do, as a process of bringing things into visible form, of bringing things down into concrete reality, and by defining a need as a visible, concrete thing, we are tempted to say that a manifestation is successful when the visible, concrete form of the need appears within our environment. Here we limit manifestation to being simply a process of materialization, of attracting things which are external to us.

Being a spiritual process, manifestation is also successful if it results in a change of consciousness. It is not having a need fulfilled that is important; the vital thing is what the meeting of that need does to allow consciousness to grow and expand. To think of manifestation only as a means of meeting needs and of needs as "things" is to overlook this fact. This can result in energy being wasted to meet false needs while a true soul requirement is overlooked.

For example, a person may have a deep-rooted sense of lack and insecurity. He tries to assuage this through possessions. By working the laws of manifestation, he can attract things to himself, things which he thinks he needs. Yet he never stops needing. There is no change of consciousness, no growth. He becomes a prisoner of his things and of his powers to manifest. In reality, manifestation is unsuccessful for him, for he has failed to manifest his true need, the inner state that would give him peace.

Further, by seeing needs as concrete forms, we may limit ourselves to the mental level of manifestation in which we must always define each need accurately and visualize it precisely. Obviously this works, but it condemns the consciousness to always having to manifest in stages, one thing at a time, rather than allowing the individual to become at one with the essence behind all things and thus moving into greater levels of realization and power. Also, the mind of man is finite and can only grasp so much at any one time in conscious attention. It may therefore focus in on a specific need but fail to grasp a greater one of which the specific is only a part. Alternatively, lacking certain data which might be available on higher, abstract, formless levels of consciousness (considered too vague to a consciousness that is concretely-minded), a person may manifest what his mind tells him is the perfect form only to discover that it soon becomes obsolete or ineffective due to other factors or changes which have arisen. Too much precision and detail of mental vision in order to make that level of manifestation work can reduce overall flexibility and be a limitation in the long run.

Too literal and concrete an attitude toward what constitutes a need can blind one to true needs and make one narrow. A need can be a thing such as food, clothes, shelter, and so forth. It can just as validly be an abstraction, a higher level, psychological and spiritual "thing," such as a state of consciousness. Privacy, comfort, beauty, recreation, love, joy, friendship, acceptance, a sense of accomplishment and of self-worth, can all be valid needs, as is opportunity. Discipline, understanding, knowledge, and training are all needs. Something may be a luxury at one time, a need at another.

To the soul all things are one and it is also part of this oneness. Behind all forms, there is one energy. Being attuned to that energy, having that oneness within itself, the soul feels no lack. It feels abundance, the quality of identification with wholeness, and knows that the potentiality of all things is within itself. To begin to experience this, a person must begin to think abstractly and to learn how to move comfortably beyond the concrete levels of life. Manifestation must take on a broader meaning than that of simply giving things visible, tangible form. It must be seen as the process of transferring energy from one level or state of being to another; it must be seen as a process, not of attraction, but of liberation, of externalization, of raising potentiality into actuality. Manifestation must be seen not as a way of getting what we need but as an opportunity of being what we are in our true individuality, thus bringing the realization of that individuality ever closer and more concretely into our consciousness.

To do this, need must be redefined from being a thing that fills a lack into being that which permits and nourishes in the moment the externalization and growth, in harmony with the whole, of the God within, the spirit. A need is that which allows the individuality to grow in self-realization and to express its divinity on all levels of consciousness and form. It is a revelation of a potentiality waiting to be an actuality, of a God-life waiting to be released, of a reality waiting to emerge from the chrysalis of infinity's dreaming. Need is an invitation, an opportunity, to the soul to be in manifestation what it already is in essence.

In fact there is only one real need in creation: the need of God to be Himself in expression. Likewise, there is really only one true act of manifestation: that which reveals the being of God and allows it expression in creativity.

Manifestation

I have already said what manifestation is. By now, through our discussions, a sense of the greater reality and meaning behind this spiritual process may be apparent. It is much more than a technique or a set of laws and principles. It is an act and affirmation of essential divine beingness. It is the creative spirit being itself. This is why the energy and quality we call "will" is so vital a part of the process of manifestation, for will is the primary emanation of being; it is the quality of beingness.

Manifestation is in essence creation, and its laws are basically laws of creativity. To be a true manifestor, man must redefine himself from being a receiver into being a divine creator. God (hence the divinity within man) creates not by manipulation and domination but through being. All creation is an aspect, a reflection, of what God is. God creates, or manifests, by being Himself.

Ultimately, the secret of manifestation is in being. TO BE is the one and only Law of Manifestation.

Its outworking is infallible. Each consciousness will experience exactly what it is able to be on the level of its functioning awareness. By developing that awareness through different levels of life, consciousness learns about itself and about the oneness that stands behind yet permeates all levels. Through a long and painful, or short and pleasant, process, depending on the individual's choices, out of the welter of perceptions, reactions, feelings, thoughts, energies, and experiences, there will come a distillation of true vision, wisdom, and knowing through which the consciousness realizes that it is itself part of and one with in total identity that oneness pervading all things. The individual learns to BE the Center, instead of the swirling, changing periphery. Through this knowledge, God is revealed.

Manifestation is ultimately defined as the revelation of this One Being, the beingness of God and of ourselves as one with Him. It is making God apparent through conscious, knowing activity arising out of a consciousness at one with Him. The extent of this revelation may be small and fleeting but it will have a lasting impact on the immortal Individuality. Any act of manifestation that does not in some way provide for that impact, that revelation of the spirit of God, is not a successful manifestation. It is only a playing with energy, a juggling with forms in time and space; it is rearrangement, not manifestation. The greatest product of manifestation is growth, expansion, revelation. If this is not present as a result of working the laws, then one may be a successful occultist or an adept or positive thinker and may have adequately attracted forms to oneself, but one has nevertheless failed to manifest. The greater need for penetration into and realization of one's own infinite divinity and oneness with the whole, with consequent freedom from the limitations of form, the need for divine revelation, remains unfulfilled.

The new laws of manifestation represent a call to penetrate more deeply into the mystery of one's being. They are based on the definitions given above. Basically, they state that each man is one with the whole, one with God. He is a portal through whom God can manifest; he can incarnate the Divine, for divinity is his own essential beingness. Because of this, within himself is the essence of all things, therefore he need feel no lack. What he must do is to BE, to manifest divinity, then he will attract to himself automatically whatever he needs at any given moment to assist and increase that manifestation. A biblical keynote to this is "Seek ye first the Kingdom of Heaven and all else shall be added." The kingdom of heaven is the state of identification with one's true individuality, the Source within, the Divine Center, that I AM THAT I AM which is not the product of an environment, not affected by change, by pressure, by time or by space, but is its own self-sufficient cause and reason for being. Moving step by step in consciousness, one learns to "practice the presence" of this individuality, using one's mind, emotions, body and soul to express in one's daily life the qualities of divinity as one understands them, knowing that greater understanding will consequently come.

By striving to relate to life from a centered state of inner poise, stillness, and attunement, rather than from a changing flux of personality reactions and shifting mask-like identities, one learns what it means to really BE. Then the secrets of manifestation open up. We spoke earlier of people using will to discover themselves. By working with God on whatever level of reality we can see Him—whether as laws, parent, mind, beloved, or a partner—we learn of our true identity. We may manifest things, but if we are doing it correctly, we are really manifesting ourselves, our *real selves.*

The new laws help our consciousness not become tied to the personality definitions and levels of manifestation, eventually losing the spirit in the technique, something which the mind can easily do. However the new laws do not replace the old ones; they simply place them into a different context. One can be fully attuned to being, but there is still a need to express that beingness and its energies in a creative way. When a person fully understands the new laws and embodies them to some degree, then the old laws become tools of creativity, rather than of manifestation, ways of expressing God into form, rather than ways of simply attracting forms.

For example, I can be free from any sense of need or lack through knowing my oneness with the whole and having a consciousness filled with the quality of abundance. I can see myself as working with God to reveal His plan. There is still a need for that work and revelation to take practical energy forms. Every form that exists, whether it is a tree or a rock, a snail or a star, is a precise form held in God's mind. God forms precise images to create, therefore so can I. God uses emotional energy to create. So can I. God manifests through physical energy, therefore so can I, seeing labor and work as love and divinity in action. I can work on whatever level is most appropriate and necessary, using the laws of God's being, of my being, on that level to accomplish my creative designs. God creates using all the laws of manifestation on each level, remaining unseparated in His identity. I must do the same.

In a sense the new "laws" of manifestation are not laws at all; they represent an attitude, a shift of identity and consciousness, which then permit the old laws to be used to a more divinely effective degree. There should be no conflict between the levels of consciousness and manifestation. Each should blend into the other and enhance the other. The soul replaces the personality as the center of consciousness and energy, but it still uses the vehicles of the physical, emotional, and mental bodies to express itself on these dimensions. The quality and power of that expression is enhanced because it flows from the soul.

Thus, the new laws represent a state of consciousness and identification which can use the old laws as required but with greater power, effectiveness, quality and revelation. Each level enhances and includes the level beneath it. Faith does not replace work; likewise a sense of attunement and being does not replace the need for clear thought and expression on mental levels. Many great mystics have experienced the level of pure being, the soul level and beyond, but because of improper development of the mental vehicles or the emotional ones have been unable to communicate their experiences clearly; they become withdrawn from the world, living on "higher planes." The modern mystic learns the lessons each level has to offer, so that he can express his divinity from the highest level to the lowest, from the most abstract through to the most form-involved. In this way he truly reveals divinity and the blessing of the Most High.

It must further be stated that the new laws cannot be used as an escape or an excuse. Manifestation does not work if it is an escape from work or from responsibility.

Faith that something will happen is not the same as lazily assuming that it will. Simply being is an illusion, for there is nothing simple or passive about true being, the quality of dynamic creativity. Those who interpret the new laws as meaning a complacent state of drifting, a non-discriminatory, non-disciplined, non-directed stream of consciousness and activity, are missing the point of it all and will find themselves unable to manifest.

Each consciousness must learn the process of life, of God, on each level of His being, for that is the same as learning about oneself. The old laws of manifestation are born from the nature and laws governing the dimensions involved. One must be master of these dimensions and their correspondences within oneself (one's physical, emotional, and mental states and energies) before expanding to higher levels; otherwise, there is no secure and strong foundation upon which to build the higher. Yet one can never stop growing.

The mental level holds great power to create and to influence matter and energy. If this power is not to be used harmfully or separatively, it cannot be controlled by the personality alone. The soul must be the directive level. For this reason the new laws of manifestation point out the nature and reality of the soul to lift a person to that greater level.

There is no conflict between the old and new laws of manifestation. They are both aspects of being. Together they give the individual a key to divine creativity, a key that will only work if the levels are blended and worked together as an integrated oneness, the various laws representing dynamic and necessary aspects of one operation. Yet at the heart of that operation lies the secret of beingness. The portal to this beingness is self-knowledge, the knowledge of identity. The old laws taken by themselves limit the identity, as we have already discussed. The personality is a form, and is limited to form-based attitudes. To gain entrance to the portal of right identification, one must use the bridging principles or their equivalent states of consciousness to go beyond the little self, the separated self of body, emotions and mind and attune to the soul.

The new laws of manifestation represent the fulfillment and integration of the old. They are a call to man to know what he can be through perceiving more clearly what he truly is. The old laws, unillumined by the light of the new, suggest identification with form.

The new laws give consciousness the platform of awareness and greater identification through which this can be prevented and man can work divinely with form and matter without again becoming lost within them.

Then, and only then, will a person begin to know himself beyond the illusions of form. Then and only then will he be given the true scepter of power and orb of knowledge, for then lie will learn to resolve all lesser laws into himself, becoming the Law. Then he will cease to be a manifestor, but he will become for the worlds and realms of form, the Manifestation, the Revelation of the Spirit, the creative Word in the flesh.

4

Chapter Four
Working the Law

We have been discussing the spiritual principles behind manifestation, seeking to indicate the fullness of this concept and suggesting that while it certainly is a means of bringing energy into form and allowing it to express, it is much more than a way of getting things. If the Law and secret of manifestation is to BE, then it is also right to say that a deep understanding of what manifestation itself is, is also a way of understanding the mysteries of BEING. It is suggested that the concepts we have shared be used as starting points for meditation, contemplation and further development within your own consciousness and within group awareness.

Now we must begin to relate all these concepts and principles to application, both in a general way and specifically here at Findhorn. How can we work the Law in order to be all that is potential within us as individuals and as a university of light?

The following is a general description of the process of integrated manifestation. It should be realized that we are describing the working of the Law, not the laws, of manifestation. The objective is not to acquire but to reveal, knowing that any necessary acquisitions will be there as a result of proper revelation. The product of working this Law should be greater integration within the individual and between him and his environment; in other words, the consciousness of the whole is affirmed and not a consciousness of continuing subject–object separation. In working this Law it is assumed that all the lower levels of consciousness are at least oriented and reaching toward the soul, if not actually under its direction. The source energy for the manifestation emanates from the soul or from a higher level of divinity, not from a personality level. Instead the energies from these more form-orientated levels are integrated into the primary one and assist its release and expression within the realms of form according to the laws of creativity.

The process of working the Law of Manifestation may be divided up for easier discussion into four stages: Right Identification, Right Imagination, Right Attunement, and Right Action.

Right Identification

The Law of Manifestation is TO BE, but in order to BE successfully, one must know who one really is. Self-knowledge lies at the root of all. Everything we experience in life can lead us to that knowledge. Therefore, the first step to successful manifestation is to be open to life, growth, expansion, and learning.

Right Identification is knowing that one is divine spirit, at one with the whole, one with abundance. It comes from experiencing life in such a way that one penetrates beyond form and into the living, single essence behind all things. It comes from stripping away from one anything that would obscure one's true identity, that would wrap oneself in illusion and glamour.

This will require a discipline, but it is important to remember that a true discipline is never a restriction, only an affirmation. To discipline means to learn, to affirm the true vision of identity so strongly that anything else falls away; it is not repression as much as it is a joyous concentration of the energies of the being into its true channels of harmony with the whole. It is like the action of a sculptor or woodcarver who has a vision of his creation and simply chips away everything that is not part of that vision, yet in so doing works in harmony with the natural grain and texture of the stone or wood.

Putting God first, loving and caring for one's possessions as a custodian would, being open in love to serve one's world: all of these are attitudes and actions which affirm our true identity as being one with the Creator. Opening our vision outward to realize our oneness with all about us lifts us beyond the separativeness of the personality orientation. We are always growing into greater levels of identification with the whole; we must cooperate with this growing process. This is the advantage that Findhorn can offer, with the experience of the garden and the oneness with the invisible kingdoms of life, with the experience of the community and the sense of brotherhood it offers, with the experience of working with greater levels of consciousness up to and embracing that of God Himself, our own greatest self. All of these offer to us chances to grow and to expand and to know ourselves from the soul level of awareness.

Paradoxically, the best way to BE is to be. To know our true identity, we must use every opportunity to express ourselves according to the viewpoint of the soul. As we express our divinity in action, through loving what we are doing, through cooperation with others, and through learning how to create wholeness, we anchor through experience that sense of divine identity within ourselves. It becomes more than just a theory.

Knowing who we are, Right Identification, is the foundation for all successful manifestation. It attunes us to the source of all, from which all things come. It frees us from the illusion of identification with form and sets us firmly on the path of liberation. Everything in life can give us that knowledge if we will open to it in the right way and see the Truth behind the form. If this requires loss, death, suffering, giving up, discipline of the little self, or whatever one calls the process of purification to the essence of true selfhood to recognize this truth, so be it. The merchant in the New Testament parable sold all he had, but he gained the pearl of great price. Gaining the Kingdom of Heaven entails no loss, whatever the viewpoint of the personality may be, for it is the source where one gains all things: "and all else will added." For the individual who rests easy within his personality, who has learned the peace and poise of non-attachment, the route to Right Identification will be relatively free of tribulation. Whatever the cost, it is a route that must be taken. Knowing and being centered within one's true identity, the God within, is the first stage for manifestation, including the continuing manifestation of one's own being.

Right Imagination

This is really an aspect of Right Identification. It is the second stage in the overall working of the Law of

Manifestation, but it is the first step in generating and releasing energy for a specific act of manifestation. It is the equivalent on soul levels of precise thought and visualization on the mental levels. It is right identification of the need itself and the formation through the attunement of the soul of a proper image which will concentrate the creative energies and allow them to take form on some level.

If a person is rightly identifying himself with his soul reality, his oneness with the whole, then he will not see a need as a form alone, something which he lacks; he will see it as an opportunity, an opening through which God can reveal Himself. It is a chance to draw the corresponding energy from out of his inner source of oneness. Therefore, though the need may have been brought to his attention as a specific form, he must discover what the need really is as an energy, an essence within the being of God and hence within his own being. He must attune to the reality of that need within himself, releasing the energy of that reality to take appropriate form.

The starting point for creativity is silence. Just as a seed is planted in dark, rich soil, so the individual must turn his consciousness from the realm of form and plunge it into the creative soil of silence, where it can be found in the seed-states of all things. Thus, the first step in Right Imagination is meditation.

With these two energies being liberated from the personality levels under the inspiration and stimulation of the primary energy of being and knowing on the soul level, all forces within the mental and emotional environment of the person are affected and must begin to resonate in relationship to what he is generating. This generally means a release of enthusiasm, of positivity, of energy to work and to accomplish. This released energy is then available to the creative process, the inner plane builders, to use in accomplishing the manifestation. This positive energy of irresistible creation affects the subconsciousness of the race, drawing forth a complementary response from unknown individuals sometimes thousands of miles away. This is the reason behind the seeming miracles of manifestation in which a person, completely unacquainted with the need, is prompted to take an action, like sending a check, that meets the need exactly.

Right Attunement also means harmony with one's environment. This means expressing wisdom in action, in using cooperation with others, in having good coordination and communication. It means that one manifests in harmony with one's surroundings, not in spite of them, and demonstrates the rule that if it is a manifestation based on divine energy and motivation, all are blessed by it.

This also means learning to work with authority or as an authority. It means doing whatever is necessary to see that the energy flows between oneself and one's environment are harmonious, clear and coordinated. Right Attunement also means alertness to take action, to recognize opportunities that will open the way for manifestation, to obey the inner promptings that so often pave the way for success.

Right Action

This is an aspect of Right Attunement. It means the willingness and ability to do whatever is necessary on physical levels it bring the manifestation about, to assist the birth process of the divine will which the need represents. Manifestation is not always having something "drop into one's lap." It may require physical labor to bring it about.

Right Action also means right speech. We have already seen that speech is a major tool of creativity. Positive speech, constructive, clarifying, uplifting speech assists manifestation. Also economy of speech, learning to use the right words at the right time, is important, for this allows us to use the energy of manifestation with the greatest impact. By contrast, gossip, idle speech, negative speech, and destructive speech dissipates energy, weakens attunement, obscures Right Identification and hinders manifestation on all levels.

One other aspect of Right Action is very important: this is giving thanks for what one has received and then loving and caring for the manifestation, using it with skill and wisdom. Saying thank you is acknowledging the whole from which all comes; it completes the cycle, leading from Right Action back to Right Identification, for in being grateful, you open yourself to realizing your relationship with the whole, with God. Likewise you realize the love which He has for you as part of Him. It is an affirmation of the love that unites us with our Beloved, the Divine Presence. This deepens our appreciation and recognition of our true identity and strengthens our sense of oneness with the whole.

Further by thanking the human and invisible beings and agencies that were the channels that also helped manifestation to occur, we reaffirm our sense of all we have to share with each other. All of this helps us to expand our soul attunement and consciousness, helps us to grow. It enables our manifestation to be truly successful as something more than a way of attracting things. It becomes the means by which we manifest ourselves.

To fail to give thanks is to risk developing a consciousness that takes things for granted. Demanding or assuming that life will take care of us, or that others should, undermines manifestation, for these are separative attitudes that maintain us in a selfish state of personality identification, chained to the wheel of need anxieties and need gratifications.

Likewise, to love, cherish, care for and use with skill the things we receive or the people who share our lives is to realize our true nature. We are one with the Beloved, the Heart of Love within creation. God cares for all He has manifested, for all are one with Him. We must learn to realize this same identity, for it is our true identity from which all else springs. Every attitude, recognition, and act of love attunes us to the greater Heart of Love which will, through this attunement, lead us to the Source of all that we are, the priceless gift of our own divinity.

To forget this, to neglect what God has given to us for our use and growth, to be wasteful through non-appreciation, is to act in an ungodly fashion. It is to obscure further our true identity.

Thus Right Action also means returning to the Source all that has ceased to be useful to us, all that has ceased to be a meaningful part of us, and which therefore has passed outside the realm of our caring and of our love. Accumulation beyond useful application creates reservoirs of crystallized energy, blockages within universal circulation, and potential points of focus for the arising of imbalance and negativity. If the Law of Manifestation is not working for you, you may need to evaluate your state of possession. The first step to proper attraction may well be dispersal and release of that which is no longer part of you.

God's consciousness is within all his creations, giving them love, attention, and the promise of growth into His identity. If we are to be God-like, affirming our identity with Him, we too must ensure that all we

have created, all we have manifested, is filled with love
and given an opportunity for growth. Never forget that
everything has consciousness to some degree; every form
encases the divine soul awaiting and seeking growth.
Growth on the levels of inanimate form comes through
being used and appreciated. That which is left on a shelf,
hidden in a closet, not used, ceases to grow and begins
to stagnate. A reservoir of such garbage, of such stag-
nating possessions and energies, can act as a real drain
of energy within a person's environment. They represent true waste, far more than does that which, being
unwanted, is returned to the Source. The wasting of
food, for example, is not so much in returning uneaten
food to the kitchen, where it can go onto the compost
heap or into the garbage to be returned to the natural
cycle of decay and providing substance for other forms
of life. True waste would be food left on a shelf, frozen,
never thawed, never eaten.

It is important, therefore, as we seek to be the Law
of Manifestation, that we evaluate all that we have,
including the ideas and emotions that are our subtle
possessions and retaining only that which is truly a part
of us, which truly fulfills a need and thus is in a state of
dynamic service and revelation of divinity, whose

essence is to serve. Our things must, as potentially living consciousnesses, have opportunities to serve. If this is not the case, then we fail to be living exponents of divinity assisting the one real Manifestation, that of God Himself, to take place. We become collectors of forms, bound to form and inhibiting through lack of love, caring and use, the growth of God through these forms. In essence we work against the greater Manifestation while still expecting the lesser laws of manifesting to work for us in continuing expansion and acquisition. Such a conflict can only result in isolating ourselves from the Law itself and finding that nothing works for us and we are cut off until, through Right Action, we find our way back to the vision and path of Right Identification and of divine expression worthy of a son of God, a Beloved of the universe.

These are the four aspects or stages of the Law of Manifestation. The question could be asked if all this is necessary. If we learn how to BE, then surely all that we need will automatically be there for us. Why is anything else necessary? It must be remembered that being expresses on all levels. Just because we learn to function from soul levels does not mean we abandon our minds. We learn to use our minds, our emotions, and our bodies as tools for the expression of the soul. The laws of manifestation on these three levels are really the laws governing the most effective integration and expression of these levels.

Furthermore, it is important to see manifestation in its larger context as a way of fulfilling the divine plan, not just as a way of getting needs. We have no needs when we are one with Him, citizens of the kingdom; yet we still have to function as creative agents, giving form to energy and assisting spirit in its process of synthesizing energy and matter into its own balanced nature. What the Law of Manifestation says is that we are creators, for we are divine. With this realization, we can use all the tools of consciousness at our disposal on all levels to fulfill this creative destiny.

At this point it would be useful to give a concrete example of the use of these four stages in a specific act of manifestation. Let us say that John Smith wishes to manifest several thousand dollars for a down payment on a bungalow. The first stage is that of Right Identification. This, of course, has nothing to do with a specific manifestation. It should represent the continually growing and deepening state of consciousness that John always has. Yet it provides the foundation on which the energies of greater manifestation can rest. When confronted with this project, with its large expense, John must see it not as a problem or lack but as an opportunity to demonstrate the presence of God. The bungalow will enhance his ability to work, therefore it could be seen as a need. Through Right Identification, John knows that the answer to that need is already within him, within his attunement to the whole. Though the bungalow is invisible physically, it is still there in essence.

The second step, in some ways the hardest, is for John to contact that essence. What does it mean for him to have a bungalow? He thinks of its convenience as a place to live; the fact that it could provide accommodation for the community, if necessary; or that it can be a meeting place. He thinks of himself in the bungalow, which should lead him to think of himself within the larger whole of the community. What is his role in the community? Does he really need a bungalow? Perhaps another place would be better. He thinks of these things not as problems, not in an analytical way of weighing up the pros and cons, but simply as a means of "feeling out" the situation, of stripping away its outer layers of form, of using it as a thrust block to push his awareness into the deeper levels of his being-ness. What, he asks himself, really is a bungalow? What is shelter, home, etc.? What lies behind these forms and gives them meaning? John seeks to incorporate the divine idea behind the bungalow into himself. In this stage, he seeks in essence to be the bungalow, for by being it, he will manifest it. The Law says you must be that which you seek to manifest.

Of course, in practice this step may be achieved very quickly, without much thought. The point is that John is considering in silence his need, looking at it imper-sonally, seeking to see in what way it fulfills God's will, that is, in what way it embodies divinity where he is concerned and where the community is concerned. In imagination he considers all of this question: the rela-tion of the bungalow within the community's devel-opment, what role it could play in the future; he may consider the role of the money, how it will pay for the bungalow, how it will pay the men who built the bunga-low, and so forth. In any way that is helpful, he attempts to "tune in" to this thing, to experience it as it exists upon the higher, to become one with it in being. Inevi-tably, this will lead him inward to the sense and source of beingness itself. It will strengthen his own sense of identity with the whole, if he is working this step correctly and is not simply thinking intellectually. It must be creative thought designed to penetrate beyond the form of the problem giving him an "inside feel" of the manifestation.

When he gains this, it will be unquestionable. The experience is like making a contact with a source of satisfaction. A sense of knowing fills him, perhaps, or a realization of understanding. He knows the bungalow now, not just as a thing but as a living entity, a part of himself and of God seeking birth, and he also knows himself as the creative partner for that birth. Out of this knowing and attunement, an image of the right fulfillment of this essence and being will build up in his mind. It might not be of the bungalow at all; it might be of another kind of living quarters. Whatever it is, it will give him direction as well as a feeling of participating in a living process, a sharing of creativity with God, and not just a feeling of attracting inanimate things for his use.

This experience should not be confused with a psychic phenomenon; there may be nothing of a visual nature, nor a voice, nor words. What will be there is a knowing which carries with it the seeds of its own manifestation. There will be a sense of having opened out to the universe, of having expanded in some way, of being in touch with abundance.

Having used Right Imagination to become at one with the idea of the bungalow, with the energies that bungalow is designed to express, then this knowing and oneness is brought down to mental and emotional levels. John attunes to his environment, contacting those who can help him, or allowing such contacts to unfold, which they will do. For him the manifestation is essentially complete. This happened when he and the essence of bungalow became one, when he contacted within and through his own higher nature that which the bungalow will represent on the outer. What is left is to follow through in whatever way opens to him, to do whatever physical work is necessary and to give thanks when the bungalow arrives.

This example is only intended to suggest the working of these four stages. It is not intended as an accurate exposition. The experiences and atunements involved will vary from person to person. Yet if you have understood what the soul level is all about, with its subject-subject point of view, its perception of oneness, its faculty of seeing things from the inside out because it is in essence one with the life within all things and its power to be, not an attractor, but an externalizer, an evocative force, then you will understand the working of these four stages. The first two are intuitive and abstract. As the levels they represent become increasingly familiar to you, and you increasingly identify with them, they will become automatic, a way of looking at life in general, a way of attuning to and being at one with the heart and will of God. Eventually you will become a true creator, able to tune into any situation and know what it needs and able to manifest that need in some fashion. You will be the presence of the Beloved, serving His world and His evolving life.

One final comment. A person can receive direct inspiration and vision from a higher level, such as a vision that portrays what needs to be manifested. This is an action of the higher level, gathering up the work of the first two stages and communicating it to the conscious brain level of awareness. In this case the vision itself represents the product of Right Imagination. The individual knows clearly what must be manifested. Yet the knowledge of Right Identification, the oneness with the Divine, the revelation of one's true being, all these things will help to bring that manifestation, that vision, into being in the most effective way. At other times the step of Right Imagination is designed to create an inner environment of attunement, listening and stillness through which the essence of such a direct vision (or perhaps even such a vision) can come to birth within the outer consciousness, unfolding like a blossom all that one needs to know in order to carry the processes of manifestation further into form.

Chapter Five

Manifestation Within
Findhorn

The Findhorn Community has grown up around dem-
onstrations of the laws of manifestation at work. The
challenge before the community has been how to
maintain this level of demonstration as its numbers
expand, and also how to enable individual members
to experience manifestation themselves for their own
growth and deepening of consciousness.

This challenge is felt in several ways. Already a
pressure has developed in that with rapid expansion,
the community has been faced with more expenses
than ever before. On a financial level, the foundation is
paying out a good deal more than it is taking in, an
imbalance which is not healthy on any level. For some
reason, manifestation does not seem to be working.
Why? Certainly the sense of financial pressure is enough
to disrupt the group consciousness of unity that is essential to proper manifestation, but that is not the real
cause. Is it the rapid expansion itself?

In the early days there were fewer people involved in
building and expanding the center, and the consciousness of faith and vision was more adequately shared by
all concerned. When guidance was received, Peter's faith
and positive action was sufficient to bring about the
complete manifestation, but the other members were

also able to blend their strength with his in accomplishing the same thing. All shared the same vision and thus the guidance was supported by cooperative, united and concentrated human consciousness.

Now the community is much larger. Not all share the same vision, nor have the same dedication or positivity. There is an increasing tendency to discuss rather than to act, to use the mind not for illumination and clarification but for a kind of logical analysis which, since it is dealing with non-logical realities of the spirit, can only result in generating "fug," a state of mental and emotional confusion and inertia. This, of course, dissipates the energy which would otherwise be used for creating the proper channels for manifestation and fulfillment of vision.

The result is this: guidance is received, as for example to expand in a certain direction. Peter and others act accordingly; however, without the full support of the consciousness of the community, the manifestation does not proceed smoothly. There is a delay, say, in receiving funds for the project or in paying the bills; there are hold-ups in work, etc. In short, it appears that the guidance is not working out or even was wrong, or it may appear that force and pressure are being used to bring about the desired aim, further heightening the impression that it is happening "out of timing." This results in further pressures within consciousnesses that further disrupt the working of the laws of manifestation, creating still more pressure. In the end the processes of guidance and of acting to fulfill guidance are often held up for criticism and seen as the culprits in the drama. This sets the scene for a further round of pressure the next time guidance sets something into motion.

There are causes at work here to block manifestation, and these must be understood. Certainly the need for good communication, trust, understanding and love between community members and department heads is vital. We must function well on the level of human interaction before we can reasonably expect that the functioning of higher levels will manifest in fullness. We must do everything we can to consolidate and build the sense of wholeness and oneness within the community itself, creating a group sense of Right Identification, so that we are truly one organism of consciousness based on attuned manifestation.

Another important cause of confusion is that manifestation is an abstract concept until a person experiences its working within his own life. It is one thing to see it working for another or for a group. The stories of manifestation in the history of Findhorn are inspiring and certainly prove that the laws do work. However, an individual may ask, "Do they work for me?" implying correctly that it is quite another thing to have personal proof.

Those who are the "manifestors" within the community are by and large those who have experienced the processes of manifestation within their own lives before joining the community or, in some cases, since then. They know it works for them; therefore they know it will work for the whole. Those who have not experienced personal manifestation may believe that it works, but that is different from knowing. They have no personal foundation of faith through experience on which to build or base the energy to support group manifestation. Their consciousness may be marked by doubt or anxiety, by personality level limitations. Often these individuals have had little successful experience in any kind of manifestation, including working, the handling of money, wise evaluation. In short, they are young and in the field of finance, often immature. For them, the community may be a shelter from the harsher realities of the business and commercial world of the larger society.

We are seeing manifestation here in terms of finance, but it is vital to realize that it covers everything. We are seeking to manifest a way of life, a consciousness, a brotherhood, a university where special training and education can be provided. All of these aspects are affected in their ability to take form on some level by our over-all understanding and application of the Law of Manifestation. Frankly, personality-orientated consciousnesses, seeing personal need in greater perspective than group unfoldment, cannot bring these greater aspects of Findhorn into being, for they are the product of soul attunement. On the other hand, consciousnesses that seek the group good to the exclusion of the individual attainment or at the cost of the individual are also missing the point. We seek the synergetic state in which the individual wholeness and fulfillment and the group wholeness and fulfillment each contribute to and support the other. Literally, people attuned to abundance create an abundant group, while an abundant group draws forth the spirit of abundance from its people. The reverse is also true and suggests the danger of promoting negative thought forms and feelings of deprivation, insecurity and lack.

In achieving this synergetic state, we need to consider the relationship between the individual and the whole, and to indicate some ideas relevant to the level of contribution and the meeting of needs. A need is that which permits growth to take place, which enhances expansion and allows the greater Individuality and Spirit, either within an individual or a group, to emerge. A need is an opportunity to give God and His qualities of being, such as joy, love, wisdom, balance, harmony, perfection, oneness, abundance, vitality, a chance to express and usually a form through which to do so. Because the soul level represents synergetic divinity, the balanced and creative blending between the wholeness within and the wholeness that is God in macrocosm, the experience of creating a synergetic community where the whole and the individual work in perfect interrelationship, is a need, for it is an experience that will help us to appreciate more fully and grow into that greater level of consciousness.

We must realize that when an individual enters the community, especially a young person, he is concentrating himself to achieve a certain objective of growth and consciousness. The dynamic life of the community demands his attention in ways that the larger society does not. His range of contacts may also be diminished. He surrenders some of his free agency in order to blend his destiny with that of a larger whole. This means that channels of manifestation normally open to a person in society may not be as available to individuals within the community. The community itself becomes therefore the primary channel through which God can manifest the needs of the individual members. This requires that the channel be not blocked, otherwise individuals suffer.

To me this means two things. First, the community must be aware of its responsibilities not only to the world but to its own organism, in this case to the individuals who make up the community life, seeing that their true needs are met. The community also has the right to expect that its cells are healthy, that its individual members/ creators are all fulfilling their responsibilities and their roles in community/organic life, meeting the true needs of the whole.

Second, it is not right for a few or for any number of individuals to live in the community and not support the life of the whole. To do so is to block the channel of community manifestation, making it harder for those who are carrying the energies of growth and life. It is to challenge the morale and uplift of consciousness, the momentum of expanding vision. Can we blame an individual who feels discouraged because, having given up all, accepting certain hardships and contributing on many levels to the whole that the whole might grow, he sees that no progress or growth is being made on fundamental matters such as manifestation and change of consciousness because there are those who are a continual drain on community resources on many levels? Some are strong and can, for a time if necessary, carry the load of draining people; others, growing, are threatened in their growth by such a burden. It is not a healthy thing to carry people for any length of time who do not contribute to the life of the whole. (We are not concerned here with those times when, through the arising of growth challenges, a normally contributing person has to move out of the community pattern for a time to rebalance and recreate himself.)

The responsibility of the community as a primary channel for manifestation to its members on all levels of needs, must be coupled with wisdom. The community can never and must never replace God as being seen as the source from which the answers to needs can come. The community cannot work against Right Identification. We do not try to create a welfare or socialist community. It is important that all who come here receive that training that makes them individually strong and unveils for them their divinity and oneness with the Law, so that anywhere, under any circumstances, they can function as masters, in poise, balance, love, wisdom, peace, strength and abundance. The knowledge of manifestation through self-knowledge and true beingness; the attunement to God as Beloved, as Source; the presence of unshakable faith and identification with the whole...these are all vital underpinnings to divine adulthood. To deprive a soul of the chance to develop and externalize such qualities is to fail in meeting divine and world need. Findhorn is a womb from which a new brotherhood of illumined consciousnesses, God-men and God-women, can be born. It must not become a womb into which people try to escape when life becomes too difficult. Therefore, each person must learn individually, convincingly, of the reality of God's presence, of his attunement with Him and of his consequent being of the Law of Manifestation. Each must learn to see himself not as a child who has a right to expect to be taken care of, who is dependent on a heavenly Father-Mother or on any external source, but as a maturing soul, a co-creator with God, the Beloved, meeting the challenges of creativity with zest, with joy, and with all the attributes of unfolding divinity blending with the whole of God.

Thus, as an organism the community has the need to enfold and nourish the individual lives that make it up, meeting their needs that it may have healthy growth as a whole. Yet, as a training center, it cannot foster dependency nor replace the inner divinity who is the true source for all requirements. It must allow the healthy growth of the individual wholeness. The balance must be found.

The universal balance is expressed in the divine principle of circulation. This principle describes the process of giving and receiving that governs creation, stating that every source or center of consciousness must give forth according to the nature of its being. Then, that which goes forth must return in some fashion to its source. This great principle has many aspects, such as the Law of Manifestation itself, the laws of attraction, and the law of karma or cause and effect, which describes the relationship between a source and its emanations or creations. Within human society, this balance or circulatory principle that can relate the individual and the whole together in a synergetic fashion may be expressed simply: unto him who gives all willingly, all is returned a thousand fold; he who will lose his life will gain it in greater measure; from him to whom much is given, much is expected.

This entire question resolves itself into a matter of consciousness. The solution to the problems of manifestation on any level within the community lies in the unfolding of the proper level of consciousness. It is for this reason that, to meet this challenge of expansion and varying levels of awareness, the guidance has come to alter the identity of the community from being that of a residential/working place attuned to the Light to being that of a university of Light, a place of training, a place of initiation. Work, creative expression, community life, expansion, lectures... none of these will suffice to draw the whole together into a unified and uplifting identity. Indeed the more separate activities there are which remain unrelated to a central theme of living, the more dispersed and unidentified the community will become. Everything within the community must become a conscious tool in the hands of the members to provide growth of consciousness. It is not enough to have faith in God as some inexhaustible source of supply; we must meet the real need which is to give God incarnation. Every aspect of community life, everything a person is involved in, must provide (and does provide if it is recognized) the opportunity to make the Divine manifest, to externalize our inner selves, to become familiar with our souls. We must make this a center of manifestation not through our expansion but through our ability to manifest the One within ourselves and within our collective being.

This is our challenge, the solution of which will solve other problems and needs. To meet it, the following suggestions are set forward:

One

Let all aspects of the community and its work come under the coordination of the college. This means that every area of work is seen primarily as a kind of class or opportunity for learning and is organized, as much as possible, to enhance such an opportunity. It means that each person in the community comes to see himself as a member of a university. We are each educators of each other; let us be consciously aware of what we are giving of ourselves or drawing out of others, so that we can consistently reach the highest within us each and move into soul perspective, away from personality limitations of thought and feeling. Let us be aware of all that we can learn and discover each moment.

Two

From this follows a greater appreciation of the work program. Work is love in action; it is an opportunity for us to manifest God through our love and joy in what we are doing, through our ability to work harmoniously with others. In this community, we do not work for a living. We work that we may grow. As we move increasingly into a right concept of what work is in relation to our beingness, and recognize the opportunities for growth which it provides, the distinction between work and play should disappear and all will proceed from us in an energy of joy and high accomplishment. Nothing less should satisfy us if we are truly reaching toward divinity and the freedom of the cosmos.

Three

Let us use our life at Findhorn to grasp this cosmic vision more clearly and to grow in awareness of who we really are. We are more than bodies, emotions, minds. We are part of a great wholeness of life, a community of being. The garden can illustrate this for us, as can any kind of work. By learning of the invisible kingdoms of life, the devas and elementals within nature, within art, within machinery...indeed, by learning of the life within all things, we expand our own conception of ourselves and of our wholeness.

To this end, the college will give attention to increasing the community's awareness of the kingdoms of complementary evolution through building garden and nature awareness, and through classes dealing with the energy nature of all life, the oneness of all life.

Four

As consciousness is encouraged to look beyond form while still learning to work creatively and effectively with form, the area of contribution becomes clarified. People contribute in many ways, and growth is one of the most important. It is necessary that manifestation not be limited to a monetary or concrete viewpoint. Some whom the community carries financially contribute in very meaningful ways, adding to the overall unity and energy of the whole, to which all manifestation of a group nature and individual nature is related.

Five

There are those who are being carried and who are not contributing in a meaningful way. While the community may and should support those who are integral parts of its collective being, it is able to do so because of their integrity and contribution to the health of the whole. They are embodying the Law of Manifestation. Those who are not, who are looking to the community only for supply and services, must be encouraged and helped either to change their consciousnesses or to leave.

While it is true that the average individual working full-time in the community has few outside contacts through which manifestation could obviously come, this condition can never be used as an excuse. God is limitless, and there is no person too isolated on physical levels to receive abundance if he is not also isolating himself on levels of consciousness.

Means must be provided in life for individuals to learn the secrets of spiritual strength and attunement to the Source. Each person must learn to be a manifestor through being a manifestation. If a person is not learning this at Findhorn, or is not in rhythm with the particular life that the center is unfolding, then the community must release him, no matter how valuable his skills may be, so that he can go wherever he can best learn and grow and become his greater self.

No person fails at Findhorn. There are those who are not learning or growing as they could do and who would be weakened through being supported here. The timing is not correct for them, and in the interests of true divine unfoldment—theirs and the community's— they must go forth to find new attunements and centers of learning within the greater classroom of earth.

Six

The concepts of identity-shift from personality to soul levels, concepts of true being and of manifestation, must be taught. People must learn these principles within a group context and within themselves. Projects can be established for this end. Groups of manifestation can be developed, focused around an individual or two who have proven that they have a soul level attunement and sense of Right Identification. These groups can have projects, goals of manifestation as part of their educational exercises. What is manifested could be a state of cooperation, a piece of work, a monetary need within the community, and so forth. But it will be done in such a way that everyone involved has a chance to learn and experience the principles involved.

Seven

Departments within the university can form such project groups. Each department becomes an organ of being, of manifestation, for the whole. It can learn to manifest itself and its role to the highest degree, thereby bringing greater health to the whole. This may involve creating channels for the influx of finances or of people; it may involve being a center for greater service within the community. Each department can give trust, support in consciousness, love and awareness to each other's area of operation, thus building the overall consciousness of unity and wholeness within the community.

Eight

The nature of the soul is to serve. We can emphasize the service aspect of Findhorn, bringing more people into a consciousness of service. This works in two ways. One, by being willing to serve and meet community needs. This might mean doing a job which is not what you would really want to do or what on personality levels you think you should be doing. Yet it is where you can give the best service in the moment. By doing it with love and joy, you give; and giving, will receive, including receiving in timing the job most right for you.

Two, the community can serve by not "type-casting" people, which is easy to do when someone has a particular talent, A job that was right for a person at one stage may not be right as he grows. He may need to try something new, to expand, to have a new challenge. If people know that they will not get "stuck" in a particular job, unless they really like it and are growing within it, then they will be more willing to take on jobs which they do not really feel comfortable with. The college will adminster the moving of people within jobs in correspondence to their growth and changes of consciousness. In the greater interests of Findhorn's true identity as a training place and center of initiation, it is more important for a person to grow and be given opportunities for expansion, than for a job to be filled. If a job is left vacant so that someone can grow, we are obeying the law of our identity; we will therefore manifest someone to fill that vacancy.

It is also true that individuals may wish temporarily to sacrifice growth in order to fill a vacancy or a need. In doing this, they will grow nonetheless. This is like the masters of the hierarchy who, given a chance to leave Earth and go into cosmic realms where they can truly expand their being, choose to remain tied to form and earthly matter in order to help others. Out of this sacrifice great good comes and the true furtherance of their growth as well.

Nine

It is important that working within a whole be learnt. This means understanding and accepting authority, and learning to use authority wisely oneself. In Findhorn it especially means working closely with those who represent the Center, particularly with Peter. This link with Peter is important for all department heads because of his position within the community and in the interests of coordinated communication. Good communication on all levels is vital to the health and expression of a unified organism of consciousness.

Ten

Good communication leads to awareness of each other and to sensitivity. We can each meet each other's needs to some degree, and one of the best ways to achieve successful manifestation is to help others to manifest. We can assist each other to discover and to express self-responsibility and self-discipline; we can help each other to discover what it means to be a Beloved, a Son of God, one with creation. We can help each other to be free.

On practical levels we can, through greater awareness, help the community to function better. We can dissolve mental "fug" by using our minds creatively. We can dissolve emotional tension by transmuting negative emotions, by refusing to disseminate gossip or negativity, by going directly to a responsible source if we have problems rather than simply discussing them around in a negative fashion with people who cannot do anything about them. We can help physically by right use of resources, cutting down unnecessary waste, using tools properly, working with authority and so forth.

These ten suggestions are meant to be seen as steps we can take now to enlarge and unify our consciousness as a group and as individuals. The steps themselves emanate from the nature of manifestation: they are steps toward concentration, right identification, right attunement, right action, wholeness. At the heart of these suggestions lies the core of what we are and what we can be. This is the vision of Findhorn. Above all else, this vision must be clear to live within us. The vision is not words; it is being.

Each of us is a son of the cosmos, a star-brother, a ray of divinity. Within us lies the power, the light, the love of our Source, there for us to be when we learn to identify with it in all its wholeness. Then we can incarnate the Divine, spiritualize the earth, be the Beloved in service. Whatever this takes in cost to the personality, in time, in energy, in awareness, in change, in work, it is worth it. Nothing less can suffice. Now is the time to bring heaven down on earth, to lift earth to heaven, to make the two one. We are the seed-points of reconciliation, of synthesis, that can give birth to a world beyond the imaginings of the past. We are the New in flesh if we can attune to this reality. Findhorn exists to assist this attunement, that wherever men may be, there the New can be also. We are here to initiate a new order through the transformation of ourselves. That is the vision of Findhorn. That is what we shall manifest.

About the Author

David Spangler is an author and teacher of spirituality. He was one of the original members of the Findhorn Foundation Community in Scotland, and the founder of its educational program. He is also the co-founder of the Lorian Association, a non-profit spiritual educational foundation. His books include *The Call* and *Blessing: The Art and Practice*. He lives in Washington state. Visit him at *www.Lorian.org*.

To Our Readers

Conari Press, an imprint of Red Wheel/Weiser, publishes books on topics ranging from spirituality, personal growth, and relationships to women's issues, parenting, and social issues. Our mission is to publish quality books that will make a difference in people's lives—how we feel about ourselves and how we relate to one another. We value integrity, compassion, and receptivity, both in the books we publish and in the way we do business.

Our readers are our most important resource, and we value your input, suggestions, and ideas about what you would like to see published. Please feel free to contact us, to request our latest book catalog, or to be added to our mailing list.

Conari Press
An imprint of Red Wheel/Weiser, LLC
665 Third Street, Suite 400
San Francisco, CA 94107
www.redwheelweiser.com